Under
the
Bridge

Decorations by George Salter

Zu der stillen Erde sag: Ich rinne
Zu dem raschen Wasser sprich: Ich bin.

—RAINER MARIA RILKE

Under
THE
Bridge

AN AUTOBIOGRAPHY

BY FERRIS GREENSLET

Literary Classics
Inc.
New York

Distributed by
Houghton Mifflin
Company
Boston

The Riverside Press
CAMBRIDGE · MASSACHUSETTS
PRINTED IN THE U.S.A.

CONTENTS

PART FOUR

PART FIVE

Part One

Part One

CHAPTER 1 ～

Far-off things

ALL MY LIFE I have been bored by genealogy — root and branch. Yet from the dark background of my race certain men and women stand out with whom I feel a fantastic sense of kin. Every man, as Emerson noted in the journal that he called his 'Savings Bank,' has room in his face for the features of all his ancestors. I should like to think that the countenance I regard each morning in the mirror owes something to the lineaments of that Richard Ferris who was Messenger in Ordinary of Her Majesty's Chamber to Queen Elizabeth, and the only gentleman in all the sixty-six volumes of the *Dictionary of National Biography,* so far as I can discover after more than forty years of using it almost daily, to be described quite simply as 'adventurer.'

His qualification for that high title rests on the meagre record of a single exploit. It is found in a pamphlet dated 1590, published by one Edward White and sold at his Shop by the Little North Door of Paul's, at the sign of the *Gun,* under the title 'The Most Conspicuous and Memorable Adventure of Richard Ferris.'

This Richard, by the evidence manifestly a sportsman, made a wager of fifty pounds that he would proceed by sea in a small wherry boat from London to the city of Bristol. The objects of the trip were threefold: the fifty pounds, the boat ride, and to give the Spaniards, who two years before had littered the coasts of the British Isles with the bones of the Armada, an eyeful. As the adventurer himself puts it in higher erected phrase, the better to daunt the enemies of this nation.

His setting out is thus described:

'The boat wherein I determined to perform my promise was new built; which I procured to be painted with green, and the oars and sail of the same colour, with the Red Cross for England, and Her Majesty's arms, with a vane standing fast to the stern of the said boat; which being in full readiness, upon Midsummer Day last, myself, with my companions, ANDREW HILL and WILLIAM THOMAS, with a great many of our friends and well willers accompanying us to the Tower Wharf of London, there we entered our boat; and so, with a great many of our friends in other like boats, rowed to the Court at Greenwich; where before the Court Gate, we gave a volley of shot. Then we landed and went into the Court, where we had Great Entertainment at every Office; and many of our friends were full sorry for our departing.'

Great Entertainment proved to be a feature of the voyage. Twenty-one of its forty nights were spent on shore, and always the Squire or other local potentate, on learning that the visitor from the sea was of the bedchamber of the Virgin Queen, did him very well indeed. Of other danger he had little save for a narrow escape from a pirate, rather diminutive, but to a wherry as a frigate to a brig:

'The Next morning, we set out to go for Land's End; where setting from Penzance with our half tide, to recover the first of the tide at Land's End, we being in our boat a great way from the shore; our Master descried a pirate, having a vessel of four tons; who made toward us amain, meaning doubtless to have robbed us. But doubting such a matter, we rowed so near the shore as we might. And by that time as he was almost come at us, we were near to a rock standing in the sea; where this pirate thought to have taken us at an advantage. For being come close to the outside of the said rock, called Raymolde Stones, he was becalmed, and could make no way, and so were we. But GOD (who never faileth those that put their trust in Him!) sent us a comfort unlooked for. For as we rowed to come about by this rock, suddenly we espied a plain and very easy way to pass on the inner side of the said rock; where we went through very pleasantly; and by reason thereof, he could not follow us.'

At Bristol, where they presently arrived, there was more great entertainment, and the green wherry mounted on wheels was drawn over the Great West Road, running a gantlet of entertainment, to London. There the reception, in addition to roast ox and sherris sack, included fireworks and poetry. Of the last a sample survives:

> Come, old and young! behold and view!
> A thing most rare is to be seen!
> A silly wherry, it is most true!
> Is come to town, with sail of green;
> With oars, colour of the same:
> To happy FERRIS' worthy fame!
>
> O gallant minds and venturous bold!
> That took in hand, a thing most rare.
> 'Twill make the Spaniards' hearts wax cold!
> If that this news to them repair,
> That three men hath this voyage done,
> And thereby wagers great have won.

To trace the exact steps of my descent on the distaff side from Richard the adventurer is beyond my genealogical powers, but after a life which has included thousands of hours spent in skiffs, small sailing boats and canoes, with liking for any wager, and some experience of entertainment, I feel that Richard was a member of the family definitely sympathetic.

The scene changes from Elizabethan London to Jacobean Salem.

There the first Greenslets, coming from West Somersetshire, turned up in the New World. Like Richard Ferris the men were seagoing fellows. As early as 1673, Thomas Greenslet was admonished for breach of the Sabbath, it is surmised for fishing on Sunday, which for three centuries has been a family failing.

Nineteen years later in the black year of the Witchcraft delusion, Greenslets were in court again, this time on a graver charge.

Thomas Greenslet dying in 1674 had left a wife Ann and five children. His estate was inconspicuous and Ann seems to have set herself up as a practical nurse. Soon she was employed upon a notorious case. Jacob Pudeator had a wife Isobel who was a scandal to the community. Many times she was before the magistrates for drunkenness, railing and base words, wasting her husband's substance, threatening to burn his house down, endangering his very life. At his wits' end Pudeator engaged Ann Greenslet to look after his dipsomaniac. Isobel died soon after under circumstances that gave rise to the suspicion that Jacob, in defiance of doctor's orders, had plied her with hairs of the dog. He married the Widow Greenslet. Hope really triumphed over experience. At his death his will was found to speak gratefully and affectionately of Ann, and after legacies of five pounds to each of her five Greenslet children he left her the residue of a modest property. Charles Upham in the *History of Salem Witchcraft* affirms, 'she was a kind neighbor and was prompt in offices of charity and sympathy.'

How and when this unfortunate lady became the object of hysterical suspicion, denounced as 'Bitch-witch' and 'Hag of Hell,' we don't know; but in the spring of the manic year of 1692 she was accused, and was tried in September.

How pitiful and terrible the flimsy evidence given at her trial!

Mary Warren testified that 'Pudeator often stuck her with pins, and it was either her or her apparition which was the cause of John Turner's falling off the cherry tree to his great hurt, and which amazed him in his head, and almost killed him, and also she killed her husband and John Best's wife.'

John Best said: 'My mother several times in her sickness complained that Ann Pudeator of Salem bewitched her and she believed she would kill her before she was done with her. Several times I went into the woods to fetch my father's cows and I did drive Goody Pudeator's cow back from our cows and I, being alone, she would chide me when I came home from driving the cows back, for this reason I do believe said Pudeator to be a witch.'

Sam Pickworth said: 'I was coming along Salem Street about six weeks ago when I saw a woman near Captain Higginson's house which I supposed was Ann Pudeator, and in a moment of time she past me as swift as if a bird flew past me and I saw said woman go into Ann Pudeator's house.'

The chief witness for the defense was the accused herself. Whatever she may have done contrary to the *bonos mores* of

Salem, and though a confession would have saved her life, she steadfastly denied any dealings with the Devil. Her son Thomas supported her without effect. She was hanged on September 22, with the last batch of poor bodies to give their lives to Puritanism gone mad.

I do not search my countenance for vestiges of Ann Greenslet, but in a small corner of the heart abides a resentment at her fate. In the presence of intolerance, mass hysteria, and the closed mind, I feel a sickness of soul that seems to spring from something further back than one's own little life.

After the end of Ann, the Greenslets, ill at ease in the Witch City, moved to the shore of Casco Bay where others of the family were already established, drawing as usual their living from the sea. None seems to have accomplished anything of note, and presently they faded from the country of the pointed firs, to appear a century later in Vermont, where a Greenslet and wife are fabled to have fought side by side at the Battle of Bennington. There in 1843 was born George Greenslet who comes more intimately into this story. He received something of an education at the neighboring academy in Pownal, and in the first year of the War Between the States, a boy of eighteen, bantam weight, crossed the old frontier of Independent Vermont to the Valley of the Hudson to teach a school of boys older and bigger than himself in the thriving lumber village of Glens Falls.

Meanwhile the stream of the distaff side was flowing toward a watersmeet.

A generation before the Greenslets had taken fish off the North Shore and run into trouble in Salem, a numerous clan of Wings, Quakers, non-combatants and astonishingly prolific, landed at Sandwich in the inner elbow of Cape Cod.

With them, intermingled in business and marriage, came a family of Ferrises, less prolific, more belligerent, and exemplifying in every generation the self-evident truth that adventures are for the adventurous.

In the terrain of the future village of Glens Falls, World History was making. Indians — Algonquins, Hurons, Mohawks, and Iroquois — knew it as the Great Carrying Place. Its fifteen miles of sand and gloomy pines, encircled on three sides by low mountains, were the height of land and chief hazard of an ancient route by water from the St. Lawrence River along Lake Champlain and Lake George to the Hudson and the sea. In 1609, Champlain had followed this route as far south as Ticonderoga and, at the price of a short stiff climb, could have looked out over another long, lovely lake to the west and south.

In 1642, the year that Richelieu died in France and the Great Rebellion began in England, Father Isaac Jogues, captured by hostile Indians, was taken the length of Lake Champlain, along the second lake, hitherto virgin of white voyager, across the Great Carrying Place and down the Hudson to the Mohawk country. Escaping after incredible hardship and suffering that included the cutting off of a thumb by an Algonquin woman whom he had himself converted, the indomitable Jesuit was back within two years to turn the other cheek. This time, he christened the lake beyond Champlain's, to whose green and silver beauty he could not have been indifferent, Lac Saint-Sacrement, completed the course to the Mohawk, and achieved his life's ambition — torture, death, and an unmarked grave. For a century thereafter the birds and beasts and fishes of the Great Carrying Place were disturbed only by parties of red men fishing, hunting, scouting; or surveyors acting for gentlemen in hopeful quest of land grants from the Crown.

In 1756, power politics and secret treaties brought on the Seven Years' War that determined the ownership of the North American Continent. Decisive battles were fought in the picturesque and romantic terrain of which the Great Carrying Place was still the bottleneck and hotspot.

Those fifteen dangerous miles between Fort William Henry at the southern end of Lake George and Fort Edward at the bend of the Hudson where falls and rapids ceased and navigation began for canoe and bateau were exactly bisected by the Halfway Brook, the 'Bloody Brook,' as Robert Rogers of the Rangers called it. On its southern bank in 1759, just after the capture of Ticonderoga from the French, was established the first permanent resident of Glens Falls, my maternal grandmother's grandfather, Jeffrey Cooper.

As his little green, blue, and scarlet-coated army of thirteen thousand men moved north from Fort Edward through the dark pines, along a road cut ten rods wide to avoid surprise, Lord Amherst had left, as second in command of the blockhouse at the Bloody Brook, this Cooper, described as Lieutenant of the brig *Cicero* of thirty-four guns. Seagoing fellows will like to know that it was really a 'snow' with a short mast for a trysail abaft the mainmast. When the war was over, family tradition in the person of my Great-aunt Amanda, of whom we shall hear more, relates that the trouting in the brook was so satisfactory that the Lieutenant wished to remain where he was. He seems to have been a protégé or kinsman of Amherst who interested himself in the matter and wrote a letter to the authorities in New York in his behalf. Both the sizeable blockhouse and a considerable acreage of streamside land were allotted him, and he settled down to a life divided between farming and fishing with, on occasion, a little innkeeping thrown in.

On the site of his little fishing fortress stands a marker of bronze and granite. I like to think it is a monument to the two-pounders which Jeffrey, as a poet of his own time put it, 'did with yielding rod solicit to the shore.'

About midday of August 28, 1762, to Jeffrey Cooper, probably cleaning fish as it had been a showery morning, appeared on the old military road from the south a considerable company of men on horseback. As we learn from the diary of its leader, together with the details of time and weather, they 'were doubtful of some trouble.' Introducing themselves as Abraham Wing of Oblong in Dutchess County, with attendant partners and sons-in-law, they announced that they had acquired a patent from the Crown for a new township to be called Queensbury, and to include the territory of the old Carrying Place. They asked for rooms and storage.

The expected trouble was not forthcoming. Though the invasion of his angler's paradise was undoubtedly a shock, Jeffrey 'after a short consideration' took them in. Surveying and distribution of land went forward, and the building of houses began. The proprietor of the blockhouse by the brook was left undisturbed. The new log dwellings and the several hundreds of acres that went with each of them were spread out a mile or more to the south along the north bank of the Hudson near the Falls with their useful waterpower. In May, 1766, at the first meeting of the town of Queensbury, of the eleven elective offices, Abraham Wing, with three thousand acres, held three, Moderator, Supervisor, and Overseer of the Poor; later he became also Keeper of the Pound. Jeffrey Cooper was Assessor.

Quite naturally the little village was known as Wing's

Falls — but not for long. Soon after the Revolution, Colonel John Glen of Schenectady, who held the patent to the land on the south bank of the river and believed in publicity, proposed to Abraham Wing that the name of the settlement should be changed to Glens Falls. According to Dr. A. W. Holden's scholarly and admirably written history of the Town of Queensbury, published three quarters of a century ago, the consideration offered and accepted was 'a wine supper.' According to Great-aunt Amanda, Abraham's granddaughter, it was 'another bottle' when the supper had already reached, or perhaps just passed its peak.

She had, too, a story of the morning after; — how Abraham, driving down to his stone mill by the river, observed that one track of his sleigh, made just as a light snow of the night before had ceased, was within half an inch of the unguarded edge of the new bridge across the chasm, and how he thereupon took a pledge which was not broken for several months. This has a flavor of embellishment. Yet the legends of the past with which she thrilled a little grand-nephew and held him from his play, when checked half a century later, were found sustained by unquestionable authority.

In the Revolution the Carrying Place saw something less of decisive action than in the Old French War. John Burgoyne, dramatist and general, by-passed it in favor of the more direct road down the south arm of Lake Champlain and along Woods Creek to Fort Ann, Fort Edward, and Saratoga, while the ordnance, the Baron and Baroness Riedesel, Burgoyne's ladies, and other precious matériel of war, were sent the less strongly contested way by Lake George, the Halfway Brook and Wing's Falls. In all the eight years of the Revolution there were constant excursions and alarms, minor attack and counter-attack, and the houses at the Falls were twice burnt to the ground.

Throughout the trouble the non-combatant Wings, evasive of the front, were chiefly occupied in securing payment for supplies taken and damage done by both the contending armies. On one occasion, Abraham himself was denounced as 'a Tory and an old rascal,' but nothing came of it. The Ferrises did their bit, one of them the hero of Great-aunt Amanda's masterpiece, quite spectacularly. This seems to have been that David Ferris who immediately upon the conclusion of the war proceeded to drown himself while piloting a raft of logs down the Mississippi River.

In the last week of July, 1777, while the Americans were obstructing British progress along Woods Creek by felling trees across it, David Ferris, scouting in the vicinity of Fort Ann, was beset and captured by two of Burgoyne's Canadian Rangers. As they were dragging him off to their own lines, David (*teste* Amanda) said, 'Listen, fellows, my house is just over there four, five miles. I've got a keg of rum. Let's go over and spend the night, so I can kiss my wife good-bye.'

The Canadians thought it was a good idea.

Not long after David and wife had retired to an inner chamber, leaving the guards with their rum by the fire, the lady reappeared in a hooded cape, 'dark blue with a red lining,' affirming that she was unwell and craved a turn in the fresh air. Permission granted, the démarche was repeated several times before and after midnight. Each time her words were fewer, the hood lower. At 1:30 A.M. she appeared for the last time. Canadian heads were nodding, no words were spoken and the hood was very low. An hour later in a crate with some dozens of chickens covered with a tarpaulin, David was being driven rapidly southward toward Fort Edward, where before dawn he was safely delivered, along with the chickens, at the headquarters of General Philip Schuyler.

In London, in 1919, I lunched one day with Lord Charnwood, author of one of the best books about Abraham Lincoln, at Brooks' Club, where to dine, Sir Max Beerbohm has said, is like dining with a duke with a duke lying dead upstairs. Luncheon disposed of, we adjourned to the Smoking Room, and the host offered for examination the Club's famous Betting Book. At the top of page one, under the date of Christmas Day, 1776, I read:

'John Burgoyne wagers Charles Fox one pony (fifty guineas) that he will be home victorious from America by Christmas Day, 1777.'

I seemed to hear the spirit of Great-aunt Amanda giggling within me. John spent that holiday at the Apthorp house in Cambridge, Massachusetts.

After the revolution Glens Falls prospered. The soil was fertile, grist mills and sawmills were rising around the Falls. Wings and Ferrises flourished. John Ferris built a house by a brook emptying into the river at the mills, and dammed it into a trout pond that for a third of a century was an object of both piscatorial and gastronomic interest to French and British travellers making their way to Lake George. In the seventeen-nineties, at the very time William Wordsworth, living in France with Marie Anne Vallon, was finding it bliss in that dawn to be alive, and that to be young was very heaven, young Alfred Ferris married Sally Wing, bought land on the Bay Road, only two hours' brisk walk to the lake trout and great northern pike of Dunham's Bay, and built the house which, a century later, sheltered my own boyhood years.

Alfred's eldest son Benjamin married Sarah Cooper, granddaughter of Jeffrey. As time went on, the Ferrises flourished less than the Wings, who attended the Friends' meeting house and kept their eye on the business ball, while the Ferris men read Tom Paine and Byron, played the flute, went shooting and fishing even on Sunday, but seldom to church. There was, indeed, a non-fishing Ferris who went to church and to Congress for two terms and became one of President Grant's Commissioners for Southern Claims, but he was not typical. When the budget failed to balance, when they didn't have cash in the pocket to buy what they wanted, fishing Ferrises would sell off a little land and proceed as before. They became a kindly, humorous, imaginative, sporting, not very thrifty tribe, and such they were when Josephine, the youngest daughter of Benjamin and Sarah Cooper Ferris, was born. She was nineteen when George Greenslet, a Methodist and ardent churchgoer, came over from Vermont to teach school.

It was not long before the youthful instructor of coeval youth forsook pedagogy to commence as assistant secretary of the Glens Falls Insurance Company, which had been founded some years before by a Methodist minister, who, upon his throat failing him, had turned to fire insurance of another kind.

I have seen my mother's diary recording her doubts, hesitations, and final convictions in the course of her friendship with George Greenslet, and have the posed picture, with artificial background of landscape and the legs of a knight in armor, taken on their wedding day. I remember the few years of childhood when we were together.

> You hid so much from him then; made the nightly-
>   suspected room
> Harmless, and out of your heart full of refuge
> Mingled more human space with that of his nights.

Diary, picture, memory, the recollections of very old ladies who were her schoolmates, are all of one piece — she was sensitive, sweet, understanding, with the gods' best gift to woman, a dependable sense of humor.

Although the rambling house on the Bay Road with its eighteen rooms always had space for two more, the Ferris-Greenslet pair set up an independent home on the Ridge Road. There on June 30, 1875, at long last like Tristram Shandy, I opened my eyes on the world and raised my voice, it is said, in an expression of imperfect satisfaction.

CHAPTER 2 ～

Memory hold the door

SIXTY YEARS after the period now to be covered, I was sitting one day on the bank of a trout river discussing with John Buchan, Lord Tweedsmuir as he had recently become, the question of a title for an 'Essay in Recollection' he was planning to write. He was divided between *Pilgrim's Way* and *Memory Hold the Door*. I suggested that the latter was perhaps a little light for a Pro-Consul, better suited to a publisher. Eventually, we settled on the Bunyan rather than Stevenson phrase for his American edition. Though the latter was used in England, I have ventured to put it at the head of this chapter, not in imitation but for old association's sake, and because it exactly expresses what takes place in a mind trying to recapture the color and feeling of *le temps perdu*.

It is evident that our hero was for psychological purposes descended in the matriarchal line. Early environment and association were those of the Ferrises and I feel their mental, perhaps their moral, traits within me. A few months after my birth, the death of Sarah Ferris and indications that inspecting agencies and adjusting losses after conflagrations would keep George Greenslet more and more from home led to the return of the three to the tribal dwelling on the Bay Road. There I passed my boyhood, though from three to five months of each year were spent in a carpenter's conception of a Swiss chalet at the other end of the Bay Road on Lake George.

Alfred Ferris's house that he had built for his Wing bride had enjoyed many accretions; at first it was a smallish rectangular dwelling of the Hudson River two-chimney type. Later, he had added one-story wings on either hand. The next generation tacked on a two-story ell, taller than the original house, running back a considerable distance and terminating on the second floor in a 'shop' full of fascinating carpenters' tools, which I never knew to be put to other use than the production of my toys. There were steps up and steps down; front stairs, back stairs, and *paulo post* back stairs, one of which led to a frigid bathroom that had been built out over a piazza. There were two cellars, one for coal and wood, the other for vegetables and cider. Over all were attics, strangely connecting. It was a house of mystery and surprise.

Back of the house was a barn, sheltering, in the earlier years, a black trotting horse, chiefly used for shooting and fishing excursions. It was felt that if really pushed he could do the mile in three minutes, like the horses attached to sulkies that whirled with invisible spokes around the half-mile track on the neighboring Fair Grounds.

Back of the barn was an acre of well-kept fruit, flower, and vegetable garden. In the garden was a Tool House — an historic Tool House. One autumn day five children, inflamed by the publication of Howard Pyle's narrative and depiction of *The Merry Adventures of Robin Hood*, clad in home-made suits of Lincoln green, armed with long bows, led by a little Robin wild-eyed and spindle-shanked, a tall female child as Little John, a fat one as Friar Tuck, a medium one as Alan a-Dale, and the littlest, a blond, as Maid Marian, unfortunately mistook Walter Jacoby, the efficient gardener, for the Sheriff of Nottingham. He was lured into the Tool House and locked in it. There, despite shouts and poundings, he remained from just after breakfast till lunch time. The memory of his release is not pleasant.

The Master of the house was Benjamin Ferris, then approaching his eightieth year. Of him I remember little except the ingenious mechanical toys of wood produced in the shop, and music from two flutes of box or sandalwood with ivory rings and brass keys. These, along with some yellowed books of music, I was soon to inherit.

To Benjamin succeeded George Ferris, 'Uncle George,' man of good will and sportsman to whom my early life owed much of its happiness and health. He had remained a bachelor, because of the responsibility of looking after an unmarried sister, Aunt Abigail, whose frustrations, as it now appears, made her no easy charge. She was unsympathetic and impatient with little boys. Yet being in the house with her was not without its profit. One had an early and deep experience of the mysterious potencies of personality, became a small stoic, and learned to keep his mouth shut about his little troubles.

Further up the Bay Road in a tidy brick house lived Great-aunt Amanda, the widow of a substantial Sisson whom she had married late in his life and long survived. Her, in the character of Clio, we have already met. Physically she was something new among the lank, dark Ferrises — short, plump, and a red-head, with smiling hazel eyes. One who knew her relates:

'As children we used to visit at her back door while she was engaged in her housework. She was far in advance of her age. After washing her dishes, she packed them in a large clean willow basket, poured a kettle of boiling water over them, and left them to dry. We children, who were always being called in to wipe the dishes, thought this an admirable plan, and recommended it to our mother, but she never adopted it, thinking perhaps that wiping the dishes was good domestic discipline for small girls.'

With Great-aunt Amanda lived her septuagenarian bachelor brother, Charles, who appears from local history to have been a member of the militia and quite a dashing fellow in his prime. I possess his picture taken at seventy-five, clasping to his aged breast a deep-water lake-trout line with hook and sinker — and remember him sitting in his arm rocking chair interminably tapping out drum rolls and flourishes with his rheumatic fingers. At seventy-nine he went partridge shooting one day in the Great Cedar Swamp. When at dusk he had not returned, church bells were rung and the men and boys of the village turned out with lanterns to search for him. In the morning he strolled in, *sans* partridge, said he had been delayed, had cut a bed of cedar boughs and spent a comfortable night, only disturbed by great numbers of very large fireflies, which seemed unseasonable in November. On his eightieth birthday, wading on the cold opening day of the trout season in the Halfway Brook, he caught his death.

Strangely enough, my earliest memory is not of my native heath or the familiar persons of childhood's drama. It is of a night when I was four. I had been taken along on a visit to friends on the Isle d'Orléans in the St. Lawrence, had eaten to excess of salmon, and was very sick. I vividly recall the lights, the rushing to and fro, and, waving over me, the large, black beard of the doctor who had posted down from Quebec.

Next I begin to recall creeping downstairs by candlelight very early of a Christmas morning, to gaze spellbound at the presents spilling over the top of a pair of small pants, sewed up at the bottom of the legs, which I was encouraged to hang up as of more adequate capacity than a mere stocking. Following one of these Christmas mornings I began, and continued for years to be awakened by the sound of music. Not by the notes of lute and recorder which Montaigne's father, from a conviction of their salutary effect on character, provided to arouse his little Michel, but by an unique alarm clock which, instead of a buzzing bell, had a music-box attachment that, at the appointed hour, emitted a merry if rather tinkling tune.

My completest memories, those most closely interwoven with the fabric of my life, are of the reading of books. I cannot remember when I first mastered the art of using my eyes to create in my own mind, from black marks on white paper, the excitement and infinite wonder of the world. At five I went for a time to a Dame School kept by Miss Marion Chitty, who remembered Great-aunt Amanda's domestic modernism. After that, schooling was irregular and memory of it a blank. It is reliably reported that at eight I went to my mother, saying with obvious sincerity:

'I feel the charm that draws two beings together by delicious sympathies, making it happiness to be with each other, but misery to be apart.'

On being queried as to where on earth I got that, I replied with a priggish precision, perhaps with the pride in timely quotation which sometimes leads to the overdoing of it:

'*The Alhambra,* by Washington Irving. Page one hundred and thirty-four.'

The thousand-odd volumes which filled the shelves of the library that occupied one wing of the house included, in addition to the complete works of Irving, those of Scott, Cooper, Dickens, Thackeray, Ik Marvell, N. P. Willis, and John Burroughs. There was a bound set of *Frank Leslie's Weekly* from 1861 to 1865, copiously illustrated by its 'own artists in the field,' which hung the backdrop of my mind with pictures of war; another of *Harper's Magazine* from the beginning, with fascinating tales of travel and serial novels by Trollope and William Black; yet another of *Forest and Stream,* with its Shooting, Fishing, and Yachting sections, and its 'Sportsman Tourist' department which was to put enduring ideas into my head. A shelf of one bookcase was devoted to the works of Thaddeus Norris, Frank Forester, W. C. Prime, and other classics of field and river. Except for *The Autocrat* and some volumes by John Fiske, and Parkman, the prose writers of New England were conspicuously absent. Among the odd volumes were Tom Paine's *The Age of Reason, The Pilgrim's Progress, Innocents Abroad,* Baxter's *Saints' Rest,* with its horrid pictures of hell, and a sexy work entitled *Life Among the Mormons.*

Finally, supported by individual volumes of Byron, Tennyson, and Poe, there was a large fat book bound in red and gold, containing some twelve hundred pages in double column, that I liked best of all, *The Fireside Library of Poetry and Song.*

By the time I was ten or eleven I had read pretty much all of this literature once, most of it twice, some of it, especially the sporting books and the poetry, many times. For prose, at least, I had learned the knack, which later was probably to save my life, of reading not word by word, but in units of lines or paragraphs. I think I was preserved from turning into a bookworm only by an inextinguishable desire to try for myself everything I read about.

In my ninth year the happiness that my mother and I found in being together was ended. The misery of being forever apart preyed upon my health; I was taken out of school, and lived for two years an outdoor life that followed the sporting possibilities of the seasons.

Spring meant fishing.

With an imagination inflamed by angling literature and the capture of a few small bridge trout, I turned to the fishing equipment inherited from my grandfather along with the flutes. There were creels and ivory-handled brass winches, several flasks of a good capacity, two books of flies of home tying — chiefly grey hackles — and perhaps a half-dozen Early-Victorian rods. A significant item was a 'Sunday Rod,' a telescopic construction of whole cane, ornamented with bands of red and green, resembling until extended an innocent walking stick. It appeared quite virgin of any use, and the suspicion arose that grandfather, instead of employing it as a walking stick on Sunday mornings, trudged off quite brazenly to the streamside, marching to the rhythm of church bells with twelve feet of hickory over his shoulder.

The clou of the collection was an eleven-foot four-piece fly rod of a delightful soft whippiness. I remember working with it one day up the Old Maid's Brook, so called from the short-tempered owner of its most productive stretch — a tiny confluent of the Halfway Brook, at the moment very much in spate. In the middle of the first meadow a six-inch ribbon of black water slid through a bed of cowslips, and a grey hackle was dapped on the watery crack.

Terrific sub-aqueous explosion!

Fourteen muscular inches of silver, green, red, and gold were deposited as with a derrick amid the cowslips, but the rod, alas! had become a five-piece rod and was never repaired.

The Halfway Brook itself was the principal scene of action and, fully informed by Great-aunt Amanda of the part that smooth-sliding stream had played in the history of both the World and the Family, I seldom fished it without hearing ancestral voices prophesying war. But for haunted thrill nothing could equal Bloody Pond. Great-aunt Amanda had always come in strong on that. How at the time of Baron Dieskau's affair before Fort William Henry, the pool had been thrown so full of French and Indian bodies that men walked across it dry-shod. It contained no fish save pout. Just by it, however, as Parkman, in his *Montcalm and Wolfe*, after supporting Great-aunt Amanda's statements as to the Pond, writes with characteristic precision, 'shadowed by beeches gurgled a gloomy brook.' This, too, was supposed to have been incarnadined on that September day in 1755. The exceedingly dark-colored trout taken off its black bottom had the biggest, bloodiest spots a small history-fed angler had ever seen. They were so suggestive to his ingenious mind that at times, but for his little categorical imperative urging him on, he would have run all the seven miles home.

Trouting brought me to close quarters with more modern history too. One morning, having been awakened at three o'clock by the lively music of the alarm, I made my way across the Hudson above Cooper's Cave, where Hawkeye, and Uncas, last of the Mohicans, sheltered the Munro girls, to fish the Mount MacGregor Brook, the upper water of Herman Melville's Gansevoort Creek. Inspired by memories of Frank Leslie's pictures to ascend the mountain in a horse-drawn bus provided for that purpose, I saw General Grant, saw him plain. He sat in an armchair on the porch of his cottage, with a rug over his knees, looking out over the broad valley, scene of such marching and counter-marching long ago, thinking, in that last month of his life, his memoirs completed, who knows what!

Summer meant the Lake. But that needs a chapter.

Autumn meant shooting.

My grand-paternal inheritance included something to shoot with, as well as to fish with and play on. At first the arsenal was composed of a long Revolutionary musket, altered from flintlock to percussion, a forty-four rim-fire repeating cavalry carbine of Civil War vintage, a twenty-two calibre Flobert rifle, and a light single-barrelled breech action fowling piece. The first two were for show and fondling, but with the others, by the time I was ten, I was death to sparrows, chipmunks, rabbits, squirrels, even a rare woodcock or partridge. Before long, another single-barrelled shotgun was added, a repeating duck gun, and finally, the gift of Uncle George, a made-to-order double-barrelled bird gun. For this, the considerable length of my arms and neck were measured as for a jacket; a special piece of walnut was selected for the stock; the barrels were of lustrous, cunningly braided Damascus steel, a material hitherto known to me only in the pages of *The Talisman*. It was a thing of beauty, and I now knew the second of the three most soul-satisfying material things in the world — a fly rod and reel with well-soaked leader and appropriate fly neatly and firmly attached; a gun perfectly cleaned, oiled, loaded, and ready for action; and a sailing boat, all shipshape and Bristol fashion.

Shooting never equalled fishing as a source of a contemplative pleasure that could be enjoyed in retrospect and prospect the whole year through; but the sound of the frequent gun in the October stubble, and the feel of a fast November climb up the West or French Mountains where hysterical barking announced a treed squirrel, are unfading memories.

The pleasure of longest duration in the shooting field lies in the companionship of dogs. There was Old Ring, the surly, rather too curly cocker, over whom I shot my first woodcock. Then came Flash, who escorted me on both shooting and fishing excursions. Flash had two natures that struggled within him. Although bought as a setter, he must have had a strain of cocker that made it agony for him to hold his point till the psychological moment had arrived. He could never be trained not to *brusquer les choses*. On the banks of the Halfway Brook his habit of barking furiously, both at bulls in the pasture and rising fish in the pools, had its uses. Once, when indulging in a sport of my own invention, rabbit shooting on skates in the frozen Great Cedar Swamp where a panther had been seen not many years before, Flash emerged from the bushes he had been investigating, tail between legs at greyhound speed. His companion caught the idea, and with flashing skates reached the open country a few hundred yards away, a close second.

Dog and boy understood one another. He lived to a great age and his former partner of hill and thicket remembers with sadness the half-opened eye and feebly wagging tail that would greet him on return from college.

Bismarck, that Iron Chancellor, wrote in his old age to a friend: 'Our German fathers had a kind religion. They believed that after death they would meet again all the good dogs that had been their companions in life. I wish I could believe that now.'

So do I; though I wonder what has become of the kind of German that could have thought and said it.

Glens Falls, with its lumber and lime and pulp and paper, continued to prosper. In the eighties, among its ten thousand inhabitants, there were a half-dozen millionaires; or, if you count half-millionaires, a score. The type was well defined and constant. Sturdy, grizzled men, with short chin beards and long close-shaven upper lips, they lived on corner lots on Glen or Warren Street in large three-story houses, surmounted by ample cupolas. The purpose of these, to provide extensive observation, was defeated by the amazing growth of the maples and elms that shaded the streets, but they remained as symbols of success.

Industrial progress had turned the purely English village of an earlier time into a melting pot. The western part of the town was as French as Quebec, and it was suspected that its morals were those of Paris. East and south was a quarter known as Shermantown, as Irish as Tipperary. With both I had my contacts.

For a year or two I fell into the habit of jumping out of bed at the first clang of firebells in the night, wild bells to the wild sky, pulling on pants, boots, and sweater over my nightshirt and rushing out, probably in less than thirty seconds, to see what there was to see. The motive was consuming admiration for the firefighting prowess of one Nelson Sansouci, from the Parisian section of the town. One cold winter night the alarm pulled me out of bed at three o'clock in the morning. The fire in a saloon and lodging house of dubious repute was burning fiercely as I arrived on the scene.

My idol was on a ladder at the level of the second story, discharging water from a hose on the furnace within. A minute later the whole front wall bowed, swayed, and crashed outward into the street. In a scream which still pierces my ears, an old Frenchwoman, standing next the admirer of smoke-eaters, shouted:

'O Jésu! Nellie Sansouci est mort!'

But as the flames and brick dust settled, Nellie Sansouci, who, by some impossible feat of agility and daring, had leaped through a window to the inside as the wall fell outward, emerged singed, but smiling and bowing!

The affair of Shermantown was of a different color. In later years, fishing the trout and salmon rivers of County Cork, I was to become an admirer of the Irish people.

> The great Gaels of Ireland, the men that God made mad,
> For all their wars are merry, and all their songs are sad.

But in Glens Falls in the eighteen-eighties they were one's natural enemies. In winter they fought with snowballs. Like the Celts from the South End who on Boston Common took part in the education of young Henry Adams, they were not above the use of prepared missiles frozen around a stone core. In summer they hurled the stone without the snow, or 'chawed' shirts and drawers and stockings discovered on the banks of swimming holes of the Hudson or Feeder Dam Canal. This was not a process, as it might seem to the uninitiated, involving mastication and the gnashing of teeth. The garments were first thoroughly wetted and then tied into knots — pulled as tight as two strong boys could pull them. It was war almost to the death.

One day, with a companion a year or two older, clad not in our first long pants, but in our first white long pants, we

rashly strolled through the main street of Shermantown.
Well aware of our conspicuity, a little jittery, we passed two
large leering Irish boys engaged in close conversation.
Twenty feet by, a half brick sailed between our heads. The
companion prudently took to his heels. Scared to death, yet
driven again by the categorical imperative, our hero turned,
approached the enemy with what dignity he could muster,
and, mastering the stammer which at that time afflicted him,
enunciated:

'D-d-don't you throw b-b-b-bricks at me!'
The hostile force left the field in disgust.

The year of this encounter, 1887, brought me my first acquaintance with a man of letters. In the autumn of that year,
George Greenslet found himself 'run down' as the picturesque phrase is and, complete with growing boy, betook himself for a cure to a sanatorium in Dansville, New York. There
at the same time arrived William Dean Howells with a
daughter gravely ill. I can't at all remember how it happened. I was a shy boy of twelve; Mr. Howells was fifty-one
at the peak of his powers and reputation, and couldn't have
taken the slightest interest in narratives of achievements with
rod and gun or the legends of Great-aunt Amanda. Possibly
he may have found my naïve views of the literature I had
read entertaining. However it was, we became oddly intimate, and I cherish a copy of Rufus Zogbaum's *Horse, Foot
and Dragoons,* a happy choice, inscribed, 'From his friend
W. D. Howells.'

The date of the inscription was November 13, 1887. More
than forty years later, I read the *Life in Letters* edited by his
daughter Mildred, and learned that the very day Howells
had made a boy happy he himself was sick at heart. A week

before he had written to the Governor of Illinois asking clemency for the eight condemned Chicago 'anarchists':

'. . . The Supreme Court has denied the condemned a writ of error. That court simply affirmed the legality of the forms under which the Chicago court proceeded; it did not affirm the propriety of trying for murder men fairly indictable for conspiracy alone; and it by no means approved the principle of punishing them, because of their frantic opinions, for a crime which they were not shown to have committed. The justice or injustice of their sentence was not before the highest tribunal of our law, and unhappily could not be got there. That question must remain for history, which judges the judgment of courts, to deal with and I, for one, cannot doubt what the decision of history will be.'

On the eleventh, four were hanged, and four imprisoned, and Howells wrote: 'All over the world people must be asking themselves, what cause is this really for which men die so gladly, so inexorably? So the evil will grow from violence to violence.' On the thirteenth, the day of the presentation, he wrote to his father: 'The historical prospective is that this free Republic has killed four men for their opinions.'

These were the very thoughts that were to be in my own mind on a summer night in 1927 when, with thousands of my fellow citizens, in the presence of intolerance, mass hysteria, and the closed mind, I stood in the rain on Boston Common till long past midnight, staring at the light in the window of the Governor's office in the State House, hoping, doubting, despairing.

Up the hillside half a mile from the sights and sounds and smells of the Sanatorium, Howells had a little box of a cabin perhaps twelve feet square, furnished with a kitchen table and a couple of chairs, warmed by a Franklin stove. There he wrote, considered the manuscripts that were sent him from time to time by Harpers for an opinion, and corrected his proofs. It became the custom for me to spend the mornings there, reading proof for pleasure, and getting the first whiff of that smell of fresh ink on damp paper that still excites me.

CHAPTER 3 ～

The Lake

THE FIRST TWO BOOKS of Wordsworth's *Prelude*, with their evocations of the scenes of his childhood and youth on Windermere, would serve for a slightly idealized account of my twenty long summers at Lake George:

> Those recollected hours that have the charm
> Of visionary things, those lovely forms
> And sweet sensations that throw back our life
> And almost make remotest infancy
> A visible scene on which the sun is shining.

We went in for the same pursuits. Wordsworth's list includes swimming, rowing, fishing, sailing, skating, wood-walking, hill-climbing, reading the *Arabian Nights* even when 'the soft west wind rippled the water to the angler's wish'; flute-playing on the moonlit lake, and passing spells of 'young love-liking.' I indulged in all of these; I followed the poet, too, in being 'an impassioned nutter.'

From the veranda of the chalet, smoking a cheroot of sweet fern or dried pond lily root, later pipes of a more pernicious weed, I looked out over more than ten miles of what Parkman, who got about and can be trusted even in superlatives, called the loveliest lake in America, *Lac Saint-Sacrement!*

On the right the heavy shoulders and peak of Buck Mountain rose majestically over the low line of Assembly Point. Further to the north stood up the dark mass of Black Mountain from whose summit, after a climb enlivened by the possibility of rattlesnakes and the reality of blackberries, one beheld all of Lake George and most of Lake Champlain. On the left, still looking north from that scenic piazza, I saw the long undulating line of the West Mountain, advance guard of the Adirondacks, converging to its almost meeting with the Buck and Black Mountain range at the Narrows.

Along the thoroughfare before the outer eye, passed twice each day, with rumbling paddle-wheels, two-decker tourist steamers, *Horicon* and *Ticonderoga*, and, in silence, the *Mohican*. To the inner eye, they were convoyed by the canoes of Father Jogues, the bateaux and whaleboats of Amherst and Montcalm, the sloops and barges of Burgoyne.

The islands of the Lake were supposed, through some mystical consonance of space and time, to number three hundred and sixty-five. I liked to check figures for myself, but was never able to count above two hundred.

One of these, a mile away to the west, was a place of frequent resort. It was known as Diamond Island from the perfectly formed small quartz crystals that could be picked up at the water's edge, along with flint arrowheads and an occasional musket ball. In the Revolution, it had been the scene of a lively engagement between a battalion of British protecting supplies and Continental commandos that endeavored unsuccessfully to seize them. After the war, an English deserter had lived there for half a century, styling himself Governor of Diamond Island and Admiral of Lake George. But now it had become like Wordsworth's in Winander,

> An island musical with birds
> That sang and ceased not.

History had already lent meaning and emotion to land-scape, but at the Lake for the first time battles long ago were interfused with the most appealing shapes and hues of natural beauty. Sunset and moonrise over the storied islands, promontories, and bays were moments of inexpressible delight. In the course of time I spilled ink and spoiled paper in the attempt to express it, but in the end was content to leave it to Wordsworth.

At the Lake, rod and gun found a strong rival in tiller. I learned to sail, by the light of nature and the reading of *Forest and Stream,* in a converted rowboat to which had been added a keel and a lateen sail. Soon it had two lateen sails which gave it a pleasingly Mediterranean and piratical silhouette. On my eleventh birthday, I became master of an ancient sixteen-foot catboat, christened the *Turtle,* from its peculiar shape and the totem painted on the peak of its excessive sail. The boom overhung the taffrail by some six or eight feet. Why I wasn't drowned in it by some of the sudden squalls that howled down the mountain passes to the Lake, I can't imagine, or explain.

To the *Turtle* succeeded the *Spoon,* also named from her shape and nature. Two miles to the southwest, halfway to Fort William Henry, lived Nathaniel Bishop, author and adventurer. He had made a voyage of a thousand miles up the Amazon in a sneak-box, and written a breezy, factual book about it. Pleased with the performance of his low-lying craft, he had devised an improved type, the Barnegat

Cruiser. He increased its overall length to sixteen feet, gave
it sheer and freeboard, and an adequate but not excessive jib
and mainsail rig. It was a very able little boat, and he put it
into modest mass production. Mr. Bishop was persuaded to
part with one of these, the *Turtle* was drawn up on shore,
filled with loam and flower seeds, and the new owner had a
boat that fitted him and his occasions, like his rod and his
tailored gun. Whether beating through the rocks of the
Narrows by night, or surging home double-reefed before a
northeaster, the *Spoon* always made her landing without incident. The creak of her blocks and the slap of the water
on her curving white contours are a memorable music.

As I weathered adolescence, other changes came into my
life. George Greenslet, after five years of loneliness, married Jessie Shaver of Dutch descent from Scoharie County,
who was to become her stepson's best friend, and established
her on a corner lot on Glen Street, in a two-story brick house
with a very modest cupola. Thither the Robin Hood of Bay
Street removed, and became, as time went on, less of a
Ferris and more of a Greenslet. Coincident with these events
came a winter of religious excitement. 'Convicted of sin' by
the pulpit eloquence of some impassioned preachers, I felt
the 'call' and determined, quaintly, as it now seems, to 'pre-
pare for the ministry.' This fever quickly ran its course. The
reading of John Fiske's *Cosmic Philosophy* raised questions
that no fundamentalist could answer, and the Sabbath-fishing
Ferrises seemed better fellows and, in their character and
conduct, better Christians than many I saw startlingly ar-
rayed in church of a Sunday morning.

Back to the Lake the next summer and its poetic, pagan,

outdoor life, I found a new literary idol in the person of Edward Eggleston, novelist and historian. Twenty years before, unsettled by the new scientific thought, he had abandoned itinerant preaching for journalism in New York and Washington. There he read Taine's *Art in the Netherlands* and, inspired by it, and by encouragement from Lowell to the study of American dialects, wrote *The Hoosier Schoolmaster,* perhaps the first deliberately regional novel produced in this country. *The Schoolmaster* was followed by *Roxy,* a Seventh Commandment story, very far in advance of its time in honesty and insight, and *The Graysons,* a well-wrought and interesting tale of law and love in Lincoln's Illinois. His interests moved on from fiction to history and in the eighties he projected a Culture-History of the United States. Of this he lived to finish two volumes only — *The Beginners of a Nation* and his last and best work, *The Transit of Civilization from England to America in the Seventeenth Century.* Published in the first year of the twentieth, this was a learned, vividly written, yeasty book.

About the time I first splashed at the waters of the Lake with oars too long for me, Edward Eggleston built for himself near Joshua's Rock at the head of Dunham's Bay, an unique and attractive dwelling. It consisted of two well-designed and solidly put together buildings of the native field-stone, one for his own habitation, the other to house a library that numbered over ten thousand volumes, the greater part of them books of the sixteenth, seventeenth, and eighteenth centuries in their original calf bindings. The low window-seat of the library looked out over a charming view of bay and creek and marsh, that changed its color with the seasons and must have recalled the Dutch paintings described in Taine's book to which he owed his impulse to fiction. It was a scholar's dream-dwelling, and he fitted perfectly into the picture. He was tall, slender, with a shock of iron-grey hair and beard that stood out from the oval of his face at least five fingers' breadth in every direction, with the nose of Socrates below bright black eyes.

His conversation was as copious, various, informing, and delightful as that of the Autocrat of the Breakfast Table. To a foolish objection or silly question he could reply with the idiomatic vigor that put poor Boswell in his place. He was the first great talker I had ever met.

Our earliest conversations were over boats, not books. Dr. Eggleston, as he was generally called, had enjoyed no nautical experience on the Wabash, and his first attempts to navigate Lake George under sail were made with a specially constructed umbrella which opened up some eight or nine feet square. With this for mainsail, a fresh south wind would, in the course of a long day, transport him the thirty-five miles of the Lake's length to Ticonderoga. There he had only to wait for a northeaster or a stiff breeze from north of west to bring him home. After a year or two this waiting for favoring gales wearied him and he acquired a Barnegat Cruiser, twin sister to the *Spoon*. Informal brushes between the identic boats led to intimate discussions on seafaring subjects, and soon, by that time well along toward college, I was given the run of the scholar's library, got my first taste of Caxton and black letter, and found that even more exciting than the fragrance of proof-sheets was the subtle, penetrating odor of old calf.

The example of Howells and Eggleston, their humanity and freedom of movement, their knowledge of whatever there was to know, the joy they both seemed to find in putting words together on paper, the pleasure they took in erasing them and putting in better words, made a deep impression. I didn't quite dare to think of letters as a profession, but lime, lumber, and insurance had no charm. Misty daydreams of the future began to clear, an ambition began to take shape — something to do with books.

Part Two

CHAPTER 4

'Winch'

BY THE SPRING of 1893 it became apparent that I would be ready for college in the fall. The preparation for it had been peculiar. Between the local high school and the Academy, facilities were not wanting, but the scholastic spirit was weak. It was hard to have to leave an absorbing book, Parkman perhaps, and go to school to read 'Snow-Bound.' The fishing and shooting seasons stirred me with urges that there was no one to restrain. Arithmetic, with its artificially sugared problems of the division of apples and the jumpings of frogs, did not attract. Geography I was to learn later by wading in the trout rivers of two continents, and studying the map in two World Wars. Geometry I adored. It was visible and lucid. Algebra, with its abstractions of x and y, I disliked, but worked through the book at home in a month or two, and contrived to surmount the hurdle of the Regents' examination. In French, and Latin, I had a firm foundation; in the last, indeed, a momentum that took me through all the eight books of the Gallic War and the twelve of the *Aeneid,* and carried me on from Ovid's lively *Metamorphoses* to the *Ars Amatoria,* that corrupter of youth.

Long afterward, I may have owed an induction to the high tables of Oxford and an acquaintance with the soundest port in the world to ready Latinity. Standing on the curb of the High with the master of one college and a fellow of another, awaiting an opening to cross the unceasing stream of bicycles, hansom cabs, and Edwardian motor cars, I was inspired to recite, 'Tendebantque manus ripae ulterioris amore,' and was invited to dine that night in the hall of Christ Church.

At nearly the same time, Francis Stoddard, a professor of English at New York University, and on Washington Square justly esteemed a wit, dined in London with the Archbishop of Canterbury. At the end of an adequate meal, as they were degusting a vintage port, the Primate inquired, perhaps with a certain condescension: 'Ah, Mr. Stoddard, I suppose you have no old wines in America?'

To which Stoddard, with becoming modesty: 'No, my lord, no indeed. We have no established church.'

Back in Glens Falls, and the spring of 1893, the question of what college for the boy made great argument. Harvard exerted her traditional charm, but she seemed cold and far away. Williams, just over the mountains, looked a good base for field sports as well as study. I went so far as to make a visit there, and with the gift of obtaining previews of men with whom I was later to be intimate, rode from the station to the college in a hack with a good-looking young man whom I discovered, eight years later, to have been Bliss Perry. Greylock was satisfactory, but the college, for some reason, did not fire my imagination, and President Franklin Carter, for all his distinguished courtesy to an embarrassed boy, didn't seem to feel that my presence was indispensable to the future of the college.

Meanwhile, I learned from many concurring sources, all

endorsed by Edward Eggleston, that there were two 'great
teachers of literature,' Caleb T. Winchester, 'Winch' to his
boys at Wesleyan, in Middletown, Connecticut, and George
Edward Woodberry, at Columbia. Then came the big idea;
why not both, Winchester for college, Woodberry for university work?

Middletown at the end of the century was a handsome
town of wide, well-shaded streets, and ample houses built
from profits of the China trade. It was on tidewater, though
twenty miles from the Sound. The Connecticut River, from
its bogs and lakes on the Canadian border four hundred
miles to the northward, flows toward the sea between geo-
logically terraced banks, accented with short-pitched, pine-
topped hills that used to lead to the use of the adjective
'Japanesy' in the days when that was considered a compli-
ment. The majestic river flows on, its population changing
from trout to bass, to pike, to shad, with no obstacles save a
waterfall and a dam or two, until at Middletown it en-
counters the long rampart of wooded hills, cliff-like on the
southern side, that gives the Nutmeg State between New
Haven and New London a second line of defense from invasion by sea. Winding sharply through these obstructing
upheavals, it becomes completely and beautifully the 'Connecticut Rhine.'

As I moved into the fourth story of old North College (O
ivied walls!), I saw with satisfaction that it commanded a
view of river and hill calculated to support the spirit in the
style to which it had been accustomed.

Life became a whirl of communal activity confusing to
an individualistic habit. Athletic authorities looked me over

very intimately, to see what I could do for the glory of the college on track or field. It was discovered, to the surprise of everyone including myself, that I could walk a mile faster than any other member of the college body. For two spring seasons, overstuffed with a double daily ration of beefsteak and Bass's ale, I pounded four times around a quarter-mile track in the dual meet with Trinity. Leg after leg the dog reached Dover, usually ahead of some panting youth from the sister college who had never pursued a squirrel up the steep acclivity of the French Mountain. Then other outside affairs, the Gun Club and the *Literary Monthly,* forced retirement from the track. Almost immediately thereafter, the mile walk, with its exaggerated and ungraceful hip motions to lengthen the stride, its demand for no more inspiring athletic quality than dogged endurance, was dropped from the list of events. The walkers felt the world was getting soft; there had been giants in their days.

No sooner had the term opened than I collided squarely, for the first time in my life, with constituted authority. The principles at issue were compulsory chapel at eight o'clock every morning, and required weekly 'declamation.' With an atavistic allergy to the assembling of oneself together, to say nothing of a natural revolt against compulsion, chapel was plainly impossible. As for declamation, I had preserved from the vocal impediment of youth a distaste for public utterance, and a conviction that it was impossible to express the finer shades of the whole truth in a raised voice. The mike, that mechanical Stentor, even with Winston Churchill behind it, has not persuaded me to the contrary. There were interviews missing from both chapel and 'dec.'

After a month or two of painful conformity, I turned up with a stern but understanding dean, and, in the end, authority tacitly waived precedents that were soon to become outworn.

Through the reversed opera glass of memory, in which everything is seen remote, cool, and composed, Wesleyan was Winch, Winch was Wesleyan. A well-knit man in the late forties, he was an attractive figure to the impressionable eye. Sandy hair fell engagingly over his forehead and continued downward in side whiskers *à la* Matthew Arnold. A long clever nose, slightly off centre, stood out between quizzical eyes and a wide crooked mouth with a lower lip that protruded as if a bee had stung it newly. The general effect was of someone out of Hogarth. He was a humanist in the sense of Bacon's '*Nihil humani alienum mihi*,' not the own-axe-to-grind humanism of More and Babbitt which excluded from humanity Zola, Dreiser, and a large section of the human race. It was an apocalyptic moment, when, years later in London, I saw for the first time a colored portrait of Chaucer based on reliable indications of what he may have looked like. The inquiring yet self-contained nose, the suggestion of slyness in the humor of mouth and eyes — it was Winch!

The courses he gave followed the main line of English poetry without pausing for whistle stops: Chaucer, Shakespeare, Donne, Milton, Marvell, Dryden, Pope, Burns, Wordsworth, Coleridge, Byron, Shelley, Keats, Tennyson, Browning, Rossetti, and Arnold were dealt with as poetry, the flower of the mind of our race, with little regard for political or economic backgrounds, and none at all for the then recent Germanic discovery of *Einfluss*. He had the gift of reading poetry with a quiet poignance that missed no slightest shade of either meaning or musical effect. The thousands of stanzas, lines, tags of the British poets that are pigeonholed in my mind carry always, to my inner ear, the cadence of his voice.

He was never pontifical, never vague. I recall a seminar held in his book-lined study to which by that time I had a duplicate key. The idealism of Bishop Berkeley was up for discussion, and an eager-eyed young candidate for the ministry was discoursing, further than one could follow him, on the theme that all was spirit; there was no matter.

'No matter?' said Winch, slapping a muscular thigh, feeling of it lovingly, then slapping it again more loudly. 'I wonder, I wonder!'

Of the other instructors, two had something to say direct to my address. Max Farrand, fresh from Princeton and almost a contemporary, presented a view of history very different from that offered by Great-aunt Amanda; Oscar Kuhns opened for me the magical pages of Dante and Leopardi. In connection with Dante occurred a strange experience of the subconscious mind to which the psychoanalysts are welcome.

In my final year, described on Class Day as 'sport among scholars, scholar among sports,' I had a disappointment. I had not, as I expected and rather hoped, been elected to Mystical Seven, the senior society to which the serious scholars belonged, those who felt that life was earnest and something should be done about it at once — but, instead, to Skull and Serpent, in whose secret hall, under the symbols of man's mortality, selected sports gathered to play pool and poker and consume inordinate rations of Swiss on rye with Pilsener beer.

A fellow member of this symposium was one 'Waxey' G., who, for four years, had played an admirable second base and done no other work, beyond the barest minimum which on balance with his abilities on the diamond would get him by. He had elected Dante, thought to be a 'snap.' The procedure was for Kuhns himself to read a canto in the original, and then either translate and expound it himself or have some non-ballplaying boy do so. It was Waxey's habit while this was going on to stretch out his handsome legs from a back seat and catch up on the sleep he owed yesterday. One wouldn't have supposed he knew a word of the Tuscan tongue. Yet, very late one night, in the inner shrine of Skull and Serpent, he broke out:

'Say, boys, do you know about Dante? That Dante was one hell of a fellow! I'm just going to tell you boys all about Dante.'

And he did, reciting, in the original Italian, a passage of the thirty-third canto with its grim story of Ugolino devouring his children, of which Goethe said, 'beyond this the poetic art cannot go.'

Sober, it is doubtful if he could have recalled a single line, even the heart-breaking pivotal line of the passage,

'Io non piangeva; si dentro impietrai.'

After four years of Middletown, I felt there was still more to be learned there and returned for a year of further study, earning daily bread and beer by the correction and discussion of freshman themes. It was not an inspiring occupation, but I remember with comfort two writers who had something to say and a real notion of how to say it, Arthur Goodrich, whose prize-winning play *Caponsacchi* was the mature fruit of seeds sown by Winch, and Lee Hartman, for many years the able editor of *Harper's Magazine*. After a year of this, I invaded the Morningside Heights of New York, to superimpose upon the English Literature of Winch the Comparative Literature of Woodberry.

CHAPTER 5

What song the sirens sang

COLUMBIA in the final year of the last century was inspiring to the imagination. Under the generalship of Seth Low, it had moved from the old location of King's College in the East Fifties to the Heights, whence its handsome new buildings looked out to the west toward the Palisades of the historic Hudson, to the east and south over the great sprawling city, which seemed, to a young humanist, the very laboratory of life. Arriving in September, 1898, to become the Low Fellow in English, I settled myself in Harlem, which added a walk of a mile and a climb of some hundreds of steps, very good for the legs and wind, to one's scholarly occupations. I was glad to remember that the cliffs conquered each morning had been the scene of a brisk engagement between the forces of King George and those of George Washington, though I felt some fleeting compunction at not having offered myself as volunteer in the war with Spain, which had somehow failed to arouse my martial spirit.

At Columbia I found for the first time stimulating companionship with coeval minds, and ripe instruction that broadened and consolidated the territory explored with Winch.

Thomas Randolph Price, to whom under the terms of the appointment I was directly responsible, who guided my rather reluctant feet in the paths of Anglo-Saxon philology, was a Southerner who had left his studies in Germany uncompleted to run the blockade home to Charleston and fight in the army of Lee as aide to that blond-bearded beau sabreur J. E. B. Stuart. He was worthy of the lines in the 'Requiem' by his nextdoor neighbor in Fayerweather Hall:

> Sleep, gentle scholar of the golden lore
> Of English speech, who from thy Attic store
> Brought mastery of all tongues that poets use
> And Europe ripens, sacred to that Muse.

Brander Matthews, at the other end of the corridor, taught Molière and dramatic construction, with a shrewdness and good-fellowship symbolized by Egyptian cigarettes, king's size, that gave his classes a useful understanding of the drama as theatre. He was of the metropolitan, man-of-the-world stock of Irving and Willis. His cup was small, but he drank from his cup.

Nicholas Murray Butler, over in the top floor of the library which he was soon to leave for the President's office downstairs, taught the philosophy of Kant with admirable vigor and lucidity. He would turn to the blackboard and draw diagrams to make the antinomies or the transcendental unity of apperception as plain as the nose on your face. From him I first learned the correct philosophical name and nature of the inner voice that had urged me on to many actions I had disliked or feared, and restrained me from more for which I yearned.

Finally, there was George Edward Woodberry, at whose feet I had come there to sit.

In his *Expression in America,* a work for which, with many dissents in detail, I have much respect, Ludwig Lewisohn expresses a low opinion of Woodberry. His name appears but twice. There is a passing reference to the 'blurred idealism of George Edward Woodberry' and a later statement that 'he taught inspiringly at Columbia, but the substance of his teaching bore no relation to the realities of life and therefore none to those of literature.'

Yet listen to gallant Hans Zinsser ghosting for R. S. in *As I Remember Him:* 'He was unquestionably one of the greatest teachers this country has ever seen, inspiring with his own passionate sincerity a large and diverse group of young men, few of whom, whatever their subsequent occupations, ever lost entirely the imprint of his personality.'

An effect not devoid of relation to the realities of life such as rats, lice, and history.

When I knocked at the door of the study next to Price's to tell its occupant why I had come to Columbia, a high yet soft voice said 'Come in,' and I beheld the object of my academic desire.

A plump man just over forty in a blue serge suit; a round rubescent jowl hinted a connoisseur of vintage Burgundies; the set of carelessly worn clothes suggested a softness of flesh rather than the firm structure of muscle and bone. Yet any impression of weakness was dispelled by a dominating warrior's nose, and appraising scholar's eyes, on the defensive, slow to smile, yet irresistibly compelling when the smile came. Dark auburn hair was parted in the middle. An enormous untrimmed mustache all but hid a poet's sensuous lips.

At that very moment he was approaching the peak and

turning point — the 'peripeteia,' he would have said — of his career. It was many years before the acolyte at the altar knew and comprehended it, and what came before and after.

He was born in Beverly, six years before the incident at Fort Sumter, of a family that, two and a half centuries before, must have taken some interest in the troubles of the Greenslets over the river. His first recollection was of being held up to a window streaming with the rain and spray of a blind northeaster and told that his father was 'out there.' A Woodberry of an earlier generation had won renown, when the rudder of his ship was carried away, by sailing it to harbor stern first, perhaps a characteristic family gesture. He studied at Exeter, and was loyal to its tradition all his life, except in the matter of sports. The only suggestion that he ever left his books is in the lovely lines,

> Flower before the leaf, boy-loved Rhodora,
> Morning-pink along the valley of the birch and maple.

Indeed, nowhere is there any record of the exhilarating life of the open, save a passing comment on a line of Wordsworth's that 'any boy who has ever skated on a frozen river will understand this,' and mention in his letters of 'trying' golf while visiting Michael Pupin, and that he was 'lucky' at it — an unique confession. His only outdoor sport was day-dreaming, or star-gazing pedestrianism, preferably abroad.

At Harvard he fell under the spell of three remarkable men — Lowell, Norton, and Henry Adams. Of the first two he was the favorite pupil and protégé as long as they lived; Henry Adams's interest in young men outside of his own immediate circle was less forth-putting. After Harvard, he went to teach at the University of Nebraska. There, at first, he seems to have been discontented. This is disclosed in a letter from Norton to him, illuminating the characters of both:

'You are probably right in thinking that I would not pass three days in Lincoln. I am getting on in years and have no days to waste. I do not want to go West. But the day after I spoke my Commencement part I entered a counting-room on a wharf in Boston, and for a couple of years used to freeze in winter and to roast in summer overseeing the warehousing of thousands of bags of Rio coffee, or thousands of bales of Calcutta hides; I had to run errands, to do work that even a Freshman would not expect to do. It was against the grain, but it had to be done, and I stuck it out, and am not sorry now that I did so. I learned something of the world, and more of myself. There is no fear of your becoming barbarous. You will come back more fastidious (I trust) than ever. I do not expect to see you with war-paint and feathers.

'It is worse than you expected. Well, so you may find all the rest of life.'

During the eighties, he was back in Beverly and Boston, doing reviews and critical articles for Aldrich's *Atlantic* and Godkin's *Nation*. In the middle of the decade he wrote for the American Men of Letters series the first critical life of Poe, and to recover from that 'long examination,' made his first trip to Italy, always the land of his heart's desire; 'the charm is that so many elements of beauty are here united.' He came back sad that the glow of first acquaintance was gone, to be reassured by Aldrich, who told him 'the first voyage is only the rinsing out of the goblet of pleasure.'

In 1890, on the recommendation of Lowell and Norton, he was appointed Professor of Literature, later of Comparative Literature, at Columbia.

The setting of the University on the Heights impressed him less than it had my more naïve imagination. On Easter Day he wrote to a friend: 'I descended the rough path toward the river, thinking of Taormina, and lying on a gray rock saw Grant's tomb, which reminded me of an old friend's description of a certain woman as "a wart on the face of nature" — and Columbia's library like a collapsed balloon (the gods avert the omen) and the whole ugliness of this man-raised quarry of New York; but the blue waters saved much to the eye, for which I was grateful to the celestials overhead. So homeward (with the baseball crowd), and the façade of Union Square seemed like a continental city for dignity, and in the company of Everett House only still was discernible the muddy turbulence of the stream of life. And for this world did our Lord and Saviour rise 1864 years ago!'

No wonder he didn't care for Walt Whitman, and found him 'anathema, with only relics of the Heavenly Splendor like the Archangel ruined,' yet 'Heavenly Splendor' was hardly too strong a phrase to describe the afflatus of his own teaching, particularly in his course on the Epics, those goodly states and kingdoms that for Keats made up the Realms of Gold.

After a Socratic discussion of Aristotle's *Poetics* lasting several weeks, the class read Homer, in English, or as much Greek as they could manage, and a new planet swam into their ken; then came Lucretius, with his unending infinite rain of atoms, his imagination high-vaulting beyond the flaming ramparts of the world; then Virgil, wielder of the mightiest measure ever moulded by the lips of man, with that sense of tears in mortal things that gives its deeper meaning to the adjective 'Virgilian.'

This occupied the first four months and by mid-year the

more responsive members of the class were in a state border-
ing on permanent intoxication. After a reveille from the
horn of Roland at Roncesvalles, the work of the second sem-
ester took us through the lighter but luscious pages of Ariosto
and Tasso, detoured through Cervantes, returned to the epic
highway in Camoëns, whose *Lusiads,* as Melville, a brother
seafarer, wrote:

> In ordered ardor, nobly strong
> Flame to the height of epic song —

and concluded with Milton's *Paradise Lost.* The backgrounds of history and other literatures were always in view.

All this was presented, not by formal lectures, but in Pla-
tonic dialogues, in which understanding and appreciation
were drawn out from the inner consciousness of the re-
spondent and so felt to be wholly his own. At the end of
the hour there would be a summary from the chair, in which
divine philosophy became musical as Apollo's lute. This was
the course, together with another in Shelley for under-
graduates only, that left its imprint in the lives of men as
different as Zinsser and Keppel, scientist and administrator;
Spingarn and Bradley, soldier-scholar and man of letters;
Harry Flagler, capitalist and musician; novelists John
Erskine, Henry Sydnor Harrison, and Upton Sinclair; that
cautious adventurer F. G. Certainly a mixed bag!

It was a heady wine and for a balanced ration solids were
needed. Zinsser found them in scientific studies, I in the
skeptical prose of Swift, Anatole France, or, above all, in
Montaigne. Woodberry read these writers too, and did not
take too seriously the emotions he inspired. His letters con-
tain references to 'the illusion about me.' Yet every word of
his characterization of the followers of his master Shelley is

literally true of his own: 'This sentiment of direct, intimate, intense personal loyalty which he has inspired in them is rare if not unparalleled in literary annals.'

As time went on, he was more popular with his students than with departmental colleagues and administrative superiors. He was impatient of committees. In short, a perfectly round peg in a square hole. The population of Morningside became divided between embattled Woodberryites and anti-Woodberryites. I am afraid I was a plague to both their houses. After it was all over, I learned to my sorrow that the question of the direction of my own efforts was one of the minor causes of the war. In 1904, while on leave of absence, Woodberry resigned and later classes never knew what song the Sirens sang.

Back in Beverly he had nearly thirty years of 'a sort of dull felicity of oblivion.' He made voyages to Italy and to the African desert, where he found the 'last survivals of Puritan good taste.' He lectured to the Lowell Institute on 'The Race Power in Literature' and gave his miscellaneous audience the quintessence of his philosophy in the last paragraph of his final lecture:

'The hopes of man were not burnt away in the fire that consumed Shelley's mortal remains by the bright Mediterranean waves, nor do they sleep with his ashes by the Roman wall; they live in us. I have made much of the idea that all history is at last absorbed in imagination, and takes the form of the ideal in literature; it is a present ideal. We dip in life, as Shelley did, and we put on in our personality these forms of which I have been speaking all along — forms of liberty, forms of beauty, forms of reason — of righteousness, of kindliness, of love, of courtesy, of charity, of joy in nature, of approach to God — and these forms being present with us, eternity is with us; they have been shaped in past ages by the chosen among men — by poets, by saints, by dreamers — by Plato, by Virgil, and Dante, by Shakespeare and Goethe, who live through them in us; except in so far as they so live in us, they are dust and ashes: Babylon is not more a grave.'

A Woodberry Society was formed in New York to conserve the tradition. He wrote in modest deprecation of the plan, but said: 'It seems to me that nothing finer could come to a man than to know his name would serve as a bond of union among men for good ends. I can hardly believe I am such a man.'

Meanwhile, the star of his reputation was setting. After reading the *Heart of Man*, William James, with his gift for saying the precise, right word on any topic, had written to Mrs. Whitman, Egeria-in-chief to Boston and Cambridge in the gay nineties:

'A word about Woodberry's book. I didn't know him to be that kind of a creature at all. The essays are grave and noble in the extreme. I hail another American author. They can't be popular, and for cause. The respect of him for the Queen's English, the classic leisureliness and explicitness, which give so rare a dignity to his style, also take from it that which our generation seems to need, the sudden word, the unmediated transition, the flash of perception that makes reasonings unnecessary.'

Poetry was surely intended to be read aloud by its maker. To sit at ease with a pipe and a glass and hear Woodberry read 'He ate the laurel and is mad,' was to enjoy chamber music for woodwind of the finest quality. The piece, a long one, began softly, with the oboe inquiring,

Is it a dream that the world is fair?

The answer is assumed to be in the negative, and the poet gives us a bit of autobiography:

> I drank at dawn the muse's breath;
> In boyhood's blossom and flood
> I bit the laurel. . . .

Then follow five strophes, each beginning with two to four lines as to his intentions, and announcing the successive themes:

> I shall go singing, blood and brain,
> I shall make music of voice and lyre,
> Triumph of sorrow, paeans of pain,
> And at every fall shall the song leap higher. . . .
>
> I shall go singing over seas:
> 'The million years of the planets increase. . . .
>
> I shall go singing by tower and town:
> 'The thousand cities of men that crown
> Empire slow-rising from horde and clan
> Are clasped at one by the heart of man! . . .
>
> I shall go singing by flower and brier:
> 'The multitudinous stars of fire,
> And man made infinite under the sod
> Are clasped at one by the heart of God. . . .

All this was read steadily *crescendo*, reaching *fortissimo* as the French horn took over the theme:

> I shall go singing up ice and snow:
> 'Blow soon, dread angel, greatly blow. . . .'

Then gently, *diminuendo* to the whispered end:

> And before the silence wholly fall,
> Faintly shall soft echoes call,

Syllabling some heavenly air,
As if my spirit lingered there —
'Found fair — found fair — found fair!

This skeleton is a fine poem. All of it in cold type is a little too much. One reaches instinctively for his Montaigne, but from the poet's lips it was definitely *Ding an sich,* a thing in itself.

On the second of January, 1930, I read in the *Transcript* of Woodberry's death. Something vital had gone out of my world! Next day the President of the Institute of Arts and Letters called from New York, directing me to represent that body at the funeral. Driving down to Beverly in sub-zero weather, through some miscalculation of speed and distance, I arrived a half-hour too early. Escorted through the empty church, I was placed in the exact centre of the front seat. Not far away was Woodberry! That warrior's nose, seen in profile, had never been more dominating. It had an air of victory. It recalled the parade of the survivors of the Guards Division down Constitution Hill in London, on its return from France in 1919. At its head, sitting wearily on a great white horse, its commander, Major-General the Earl of Cavan, showed that identical profile.

For thirty minutes I meditated on the life I had touched at only one point and briefly, but which I had, I think, come to understand. There were no wife and children to miss Woodberry. The *élan vital* which finds its source and expression in the life of the family, he had never known. The mourners, when they came, were old people, soon to follow him. That fighting profile had found its field of battle in conquering misunderstanding, loneliness, and discouragement; but perhaps it was by its power he had left that imprint of himself in a hundred hearts.

Driving back to Boston, the mercury dropping still lower and my spirits *pari passu,* there flashed into my mind the remark of Edward Fitzgerald riding home from the obsequies of another difficult poet and critic, 'Poor Matt, he won't like God.'

Woodberry was a curious inquirer in odd corners of literature and it was he who suggested that my doctoral dissertation might take the form of a biography of Joseph Glanvill, an English worthy of the seventeenth century, chiefly known to fame as the source of the motto to Poe's *Ligeia* and, from the reference by Arnold to 'Glanvill's book,' for the story of *The Scholar Gypsy.*

Two years of investigations in old calf-bound volumes, assembled from abroad by an obliging librarian, the father of the author of *The Bent Twig,* together with many already in Edward Eggleston's collection at Joshua's Rock, disclosed an engaging character quite other than the 'grave Glanvill' of the poet's phrase.

A brisk, eager, inquiring, downright young man, he died at forty-four. A fashionable preacher in the Abbey Church at Bath, with white gloves and handkerchief and periwig 'that must now and then be pulled,' chaplain in ordinary to Charles the Second; at twenty-nine a member of the Royal Society, the centre of a group — resembling the Psychical Research Society of our own time — to investigate witchcraft as evidence of the spirit life; an innovator in English prose, who believed it 'an innocent way of entertaining a man's self to paint the image of his thoughts,' he provided the perfect workout for an enterprising young humanist. He was even of interest to an observer of the fighting spirit. To no less a person than Andrew Marvell, whose *Rehearsal Transprosed* satirized Glanvill's friend Samuel Parker and other puritanical parsons for facile conformity at the Restoration, he wrote in a letter: 'If thou darest publish any lie or libel against Dr. Parker, by the Eternal God I will cut thy throat.' Unterrified, Marvell published an augmented edition with the above sentence on the title page —and survived.

Glanvill's first and best book, *Vanity of Dogmatizing*, published in the year of the Restoration, was larded with happy sentences: 'The race of man is like a falling torch: though the grosser materials hasten to their element yet the flame aspires'; or, 'He is a wonderful man who can thread a needle while he is at cudgels in a crowd; and yet this is as easy as to find *Truth* in the hurry of disputation.'

His forecast of the electric telegraph by the use of 'sympathetic needles' was duly reported, but, writing before Marconi, I noted but failed to print another more astonishing prediction: 'The time will come and that presently when by making use of the magnetic waves which permeate the ether which surrounds our world we shall communicate with the Antipodes!'

Today I can hardly understand a word of my own learned chapters on 'The Cambridge Platonists' and 'Latitudinarian Theology,' but hope I did when I wrote them. *Glanvill* was published by Macmillan as Volume One in the series of Columbia Studies in English, and secured the desired doctorate. Better than that, the book was fun to write. It brought the unspeakable pleasure of a correspondence with one whom I greatly admired, Lowell's English friend Sir Leslie Stephen, editor of the *Dictionary of National Biography*, author of the learned and wise *Essays of a Biographer*, and father of

Virginia Woolf. It had a much better press than it deserved. I still wonder how a Gallic critic, writing in a learned French review, found in the youthful, slightly pedantic style, '*des intonations caressantes.*'

In June, 1900, I was hooded for the second time. On the platform, to be adorned much more resplendently, was another preview, Lord Pauncefote, the British Ambassador whose *Life and Letters* I was to publish twenty-nine years later.

The following evening the D. & H. train, having accomplished the first six miles of the Great Carrying Place north from Fort Edward, pulled panting into the Glens Falls Station. As I reached for the suitcase containing a third sheepskin and the proofs of *Glanvill,* sounds were heard of a brass band playing that inspiring melody, 'Hail to the chief who in triumph advances.'

A split second's wild surmise! Could it be — ? But before the train came to a full stop, a tall fellow traveller emerged from the smoking car and was borne off on the shoulders of a shouting, jostling crowd to a waiting barouche. Young Harry Elkes, who had won a six days' bicycle race at Madison Square Garden!

CHAPTER 6

Free lance

A YOUNG NOVELIST-TEACHER-POET of today sings of professors in patient, sedentary pants who count the commas of romance. The image haunts me with the terror of a narrow escape. Before leaving Columbia, I had been offered and had accepted a chair of English in the University of Texas. In the summer, at the Lake, I became afflicted with the recurrent family ailment of being run down, too many books, too few fish, and medical authority ordered a year of an unconfining life. Excuses and regrets were sent to Austin and the vacant chair in the heart of Texas was soon much better filled by Stark Young, who certainly never became a counter of commas.

Then came the problem, how touch the money to be unconfined with? In New York I had earned a few fairly honest dollars by reviews and articles in the *Times*, the *Forum*, and Royal Cortissoz's book page in the *Tribune*. Why not take on more of this pleasant work that could be carried around to any attractive and seasonable spot. For a reviewer who wanted to quote Latin when he felt like it, there was only one market in America, the *Nation*. I made a flying trip to New York in the muggy August weather, saw Wendell

Phillips Garrison, son of the abolitionist, and made an arrangement which gave me a new mentor, and provided me, still *en garçon,* with an income, modest but enough for the two best things money can buy — ease of mind and freedom of movement. I cherish a scrapbook containing more than five hundred *Nation* columns, as spiced with Latin as a Virginia ham with cloves.

The old *Nation* had a distinguished line of sub-editors, Hammond Lamont, the brilliant literary brother of Thomas, Frank Mather, Paul Elmer More; but Garrison, who had been literary editor under Godkin and liked it, kept dealings with his staff reviewers in his own hands. To visit his office was like a cool drink on a hot day. In the bedlam of newspaper premises his desk was an island of studious calm. Bald head, round beard, and a chronic eye trouble affecting the lower lids, gave him the look of a bust of Aeschylus, which sensitive human perceptions, clothed in a somewhat stately courtesy, did not belie. His letters were small pieces of his authentic self. He must have written scores of them by hand every working day. They were short and to the point; he never, or hardly ever, turned the page, yet none was without some vital word that instructed, chastened, or inspired the contributor. He seldom edited copy by addition or subtraction; but by his subtle guidance, by his just being there, the *Nation* read as if written by a single superman of learning and experience, able to discourse *de omni scibile et quibusdam aliis.* He encouraged and secured enough urbanity and humor, usually ironic understatement, to modulate the characteristic tone just short of the pontifical.

After three years of reviewing books of biography, literary scholarship, and belles-lettres, I took over the poetry from Colonel Thomas Wentworth Higginson, who had dealt with it for Godkin since the founding of the paper during the Civil War. The Colonel, after forty years, felt that he might put up his gun, having shot men enough; the lives of the ladies he had usually spared. One indeed was a DISCOVERY that any critic might be proud to have engraved on his monument, the wise hermit thrush of Amherst, Emily Dickinson.

For five years I was, as an old poet has it,

> Up to the chin in the Pierian flood.

Four times a year arrived by express a package containing fifty or more thin books of verse, most of them published at the author's expense by Boston's Badger. In one of his rare interpolations, Garrison inserted after this imprint the doubtfully actionable phrase *nomen est omen*. Four times a year in five or six columns I dealt with this singing spate as faithfully as I knew how. But it was Indian Summer, not only in New England, but in other quarters where the preceding summer had been less glorious, in New York and Chicago and the deep South and London, in all the federated states of Parnassus. The parade of the poets reviewed tells its tale.

In the lead stalked Yeats, Moody, Richard Hovey; next, in carriages, came Aldrich, Riley, Gilder, Stedman, Thomas Hardy, Alfred Austen, Henry van Dyke, Austin Dobson, William Watson, Watts-Dunton, Woodberry; then, marching stoutly behind, Robinson, George Cabot Lodge, Frank Dempster Sherman, Cale Young Rice, Madison Cawein, George Sterling, Gamaliel Bradford, Stephen Phillips, Ernest Dowson, Lionel Johnson, Percy MacKaye, Sturge Moore, Anna Hampstead Branch, Helen Hay Whitney, Josephine Preston Peabody, Louise Imogen Guiney, Laurence Hope, Alfred Noyes, Father Tabb, Arthur Davison Ficke, and, in the shavetail position, George Sylvester Viereck. I regret that I left the reviewing stand of the *Nation* too early to hail the advance guard of the brave new army led by Robert Frost and Edna Millay, or to salute the drums and trampling of Amy Lowell and the Imagists.

In 1908, after the death of Garrison and after I had turned publisher, I had a finger in the publication of his *Letters and Memorials.* There for the first time was printed a list of the noble company of the *Nation's* contributors. It was great to see oneself in such society, but the day was spoiled when the first bound copy came in from the Press. It opened automatically at a page whence, in a letter from Garrison to Lord Bryce, leaped to my horrified eye, '*The incomparable poof reading of the Riverside Press.*'

Life as a free-lance reviewer, or perhaps *franc-tireur* is nearer the right word, was delightful and eupeptic. As the first winter out of Columbia drew on, I found myself, so far from being run down, decidedly wound up, and ready for another adventure between covers. A sewing table was put up in the second-floor front of the brick house with a cupola on the corner lot on Glen Street — how distant from the sweet city of the dreaming spires! — and there was composed opus number two, a brief biography of Walter Pater, the first to appear. It aimed to be an appreciation like one of Pater's own, the 'purely aesthetic disengagement and reproduction of an author's aroma or bouquet.' As such, it was not too bad. Perhaps spatial distance gave it a little of the perspective of posterity. Edward Dowden of Dublin wrote of it:

'The little book is really a large one, as in big advertisements of a certain preparation for making soup a huge ox stands near a little jar which is his equal in nutriment.'

The huge ox appeared later in the bi-voluminous biography by Thomas Wright, of Olney, which Pater's heirs and Literary Executor tried in vain to prevent. It consisted of a thousand pages of irrelevant detail, and seventy-eight pages of pictures, including three of the northeast, the northwest, and the southwest corners of Pater's drawing room at Camberwell, and one of his little dog Tiny. The material was provided by a well-to-do old gentleman who after Pater's death became convinced that he himself had been the original of *Marius the Epicurean.* I reviewed it in the *Nation,* rather sadistically, I am afraid, as the failure of the Boswellian method in biography when applied by a man not a Boswell to a subject not a Johnson. As the jar was made to say to the ox in the advertisement mentioned by Dowden, 'Alas, my poor brother!'

But Pater and much that interested him, and many of the things that he stood for, have ill survived two World Wars and the internal combustion engine. I am glad now to see that the appreciation played up the subtile scholarship of *Marius* and *Plato and Platonism,* and played down Florian Deleal and Emerald Uthwart, with their faintly hermaphroditic bouquet — the fragrance that fired the greenery-yallery, Grosvenor Gallery, foot-in-the-grave young men; glad, too, that I confessed, after some months of unrelieved intimacy with the Paterian product, that I yearned for the lusty company of Sancho Panza and Tom Jones. Recently, I have been reading Santayana just after Pater's *The Renaissance.* The mourning dove is an appealing bird, but the eagle flies higher.

The heart of Pater was in his true humanism. There is no better, broader statement of its enduring essence than the last paragraph of the essay on Pico della Mirandola, golden-headed boy of Florence in the *cinque cento*:

'Nothing which has ever interested living men and women can wholly lose its vitality — no language they have spoken, no oracle beside which they have hushed their voices, no dream that has ever been entertained by actual human minds, nothing about which they have ever been passionate or expended time and zeal.'

Pater polished off, I went down to New York and established myself for the balance of the winter in the first simonpure, premeditated Bachelor Apartment built in this country, the "Benedick" on the East side of Washington Square. It seems in romantic memory to have been the true good life; a couple of hours writing for the *Nation* in the morning, then to lunch across the Square and up the Avenue swinging the stick I had taken on as emblem and evidence of frankshooting, and have never abandoned. After lunch there would be a visit to the Astor, Lenox, or Columbia Libraries to check up on the scholarship of some unfortunate whose book I was currently reviewing, then a big brisk walk in the Park or along the banks of my native river; then dinner with whomever offered, topping off with an evening at the theatre; or beer, conversation, and song; or, these failing, reading, and so to bed!

One day in the spring came a startling telegram. Uncle George, supposedly in rude outdoor health, had died suddenly — the serpent in the breast! The news was worse than sorrowful; it had elements of the tragic. He had at last, when over sixty, contracted a thoroughly suitable engagement of marriage with a summer neighbor at the Lake. Those that loved him had hoped for him a decade or more of the happiness he deserved. When his administrator looked into his affairs, it appeared at first that his assets, chiefly house property, were substantial. On further investigation, mortgages, rents remitted, and uncollectible loans to needy undesirables consumed all but a minor fraction of the estate. It took a tougher financial character than the Ferrises possessed to be at once men of good will and successful accumulators of net. The radius of the free lance's freedom of movement was slightly lengthened, but it gave him no joy.

The following autumn, after a reunion of Woodberryites at Alexandria Bay, enlivened by bass fishing and one-class boat-racing, and a bookish summer at the Lake, came a first visit to the coast of Maine, where, as a solitary passenger aboard the ninety-foot schooner *Effort,* bound from Boothbay Harbor to Monhegan Island thirty miles out to sea, I had my biggest nautical night. At dusk, soon after starting, the captain, prostrated by the world's worst colic, said, 'You'll have to take her,' and exited, groaning. All night, aided in going about by the single deckhand fresh from some Swedish farm, the skipper of the *Spoon,* with swelling chest, stood at the wheel, steering by compass, trying to make the most of a three-knot breeze that slid him softly up and down heavy ground swells, over a misty moonlit sea. Just before dawn he raised the Monhegan cliffs and a pale captain came up from below and took her in.

On my way back through Boston, I dropped in at the Public Library to pay my respects to Lindsay Swift, the Library's editor, and historian of Brook Farm. So simply do the Fates contrive the turning points in our lives.

After the customary exchange of compliments, Swift said: 'Look here, I think you are the man we are looking for. We've just bought a lot of Old French and Medieval Latin manuscripts at the Ashburnham sale in London and we can't read them. Won't you take the job of cataloguing them?' The word 'manuscript' had for my ears a compelling charm it has never lost. Within a week I had taken the required civil service examination, was installed at a desk in the Catalogue Room, drawing a salary of fifteen dollars a week; and had become, for the rest of my life, with no warning, intention, or spiritual preparation, a Bostonian.

First impressions of the town were the reverse of Puritanical or, at least, that Puritanism was spotty. In my alien innocence I had taken two rooms and bath next to a ladies' gymnasium, on a street that livened up strangely after dark. In the Library itself, with its mixed staff, I was surprised to hear from dark corners in the stacks murmurings and little squealings that were familiar in Central Park, but unexpected in the B.P.L. This was more than forty years ago. Doubtless it's different now. Perhaps the Inferno, the room where all the 'unpleasant' bad books were kept under lock and key, and exerted a malign influence, like an unexploded time bomb, is now wholesomely open to access.

An informal lunch club met every day around a table at the Victoria, in a basement so far below the level of the street that one looking up could sometimes see even the scalloped tops of passing ladies' shoes. It was a gathering of literary leftists, Hunt and Chevalier from the Library, Professor Wiener and once in a while Lanman from Harvard, Truman H. Bartlett, sculptor, Ralph Cram, Prior of the Order of the White Rose, Tom Meteyard, amateur of all the arts, the partners of the minor publishing houses of Small and Maynard, Curtis and Cameron, and Copeland and Day, who were convinced that they, not Little and Brown and Houghton and Mifflin over on the hill, were carrying the torch of

Boston letters. They were, too, up to a point. Sometimes Richard Hovey would come in, black-coated, black-hatted, black-bearded, a revenant from the Boulevards of Paris; or Bliss Carman, down from Fredericton, to read some Anacreontic just finished, to inquire whether it were suitable for *Songs from Vagabondia.* I recall a particularly agreeable one, beginning:

> Who is this I cannot see,
> Tumbling softly over me?

and my regret when it was decided to be suitable but not possible.

Not for long was I to enjoy this Bohemian atmosphere. At the end of eight weeks, just as the catalogue of the manuscripts was completed and, as a punishment perfectly fitting the crime of absences from church and chapel, I had analyzed and catalogued the contents of the seventy volumes of Migne's *Patrologiae Cursus Completus,* I was invited by the old and honorable Boston *Advertiser* to become its literary columnist. It was a step up in both pay and free time. I accepted with pleasure, but connection with the Fourth Estate lasted less than a month. While at the Library, I had written a couple of papers for the *Atlantic Monthly,* an essay on Jane Austen and an article on the English *Dictionary of National Biography,* which had just been completed. One morning I found on my desk at the *Advertiser* office — still charred from a fire the year before and never refinished — a note from Bliss Perry. If I would consider becoming sub-editor of the *Atlantic,* would I look in on him that afternoon? Would I?

Part Three

———————

CHAPTER 7

Park Street

DURING THREE MONTHS in Boston I had read local history. As I rounded windswept Brimstone Corner, where Tom Appleton suggested a shorn lamb should be permanently tethered, passed under Peter Bonner's spire that Henry James called perfectly felicitous, and gazed up the brief acclivity of Park Street to the golden dome of the Bulfinch State House, my heart swelled with the sentiment of the past. To port, spread the Common, where, through three centuries, the history of the town had unrolled *coram populo,* where all could see. To starboard, the row of red-brick Late-Georgian dwellings had housed not merely Boston's best, but her very best. John Lothrop Motley, United States Minister to Austria and England, historian of the Dutch Republic; the Quincys, Edmund and Josiah; mayors, presidents of Harvard, polished writers, leading citizens. At the top, facing the State House, stood, four-square, the mansion of the great George Ticknor. I had read Ticknor's *Letters and Journals,* and could see in my mind's eye the long library, dominated by the bust of Scott, where he had written his monumental *History of Spanish Literature,* still held in high regard on Morningside, and where he had corresponded intimately with

Presidents of the United States and leading authors of England, France, Germany, Italy, and Spain; even more intimately with numerous Duchesses and one King — the studious John of Saxony.

Turning in halfway up the hill, I climbed two flights of stairs and found myself in the engaging presence of my old chance companion of the hack, Bliss Perry. B. P., as he was called in the office, was something new in *Atlantic* editors. He had forsaken the Neptunian beard of Lowell, Fields, and Scudder, even the important mustache of Howells, Page, and Aldrich, the last with points waxed as fine as the points of his epigrams. He had returned to an earlier, more classic, New England model; he was, in short, clean-shaven. This in those days gave a literary man a notable distinction. He was more of an outdoor man than any editor since Lowell, not a superior rifle shot like J. R. L., but the champion of fishing with the worm, and not with worm only. I observed with pleasure a bag of golf clubs behind the door, not to leap too obviously to the eyes of partners arriving for the weekly Pow-Wow. With less interest in politics and the world's work than Walter Page, his immediate predecessor, he was achieving for the magazine a kind of ripe academic humanism, warmed by a note of mellow good-fellowship with contributors and subscribers alike. It did not take long for B. P. and F. G. to come to an understanding and, in less time than it takes to tell it, I was signed on to occupy that observation post, looking out over Boston Common, which, with one remove from Number Four down to Number Two, I have occupied for four decades of peace and war, and peace again, and war.

As I walked on air toward the stairs, I heard from a small darkened back room looking out on the Old Granary Burying Ground, where lie the bones of Benjamin Franklin's father and mother, and of the author of Mother Goose, a loud, contented purring. Peering in, I saw the office cat reposing in great comfort in the commodious lap of a stately old lady sound asleep. Next Monday morning, soon after eight-thirty, when I performed the classic gesture of hanging up the hat, she was there, very wide awake, and I was presented to Miss Susan Francis, who became a Great-aunt Amanda for Park Street history. Forty years before — a good-looking and clever girl she must have been, too — she had been reader for James T. Fields. She had known all the sub-editors and was not disposed to idealize them.

The first was Francis H. Underwood, who had been leg-man between Harriet Beecher Stowe and her publishers, Jewett and Company, who had thought of the *Atlantic* and put it through, been promoted after two years to be Clerk of the Superior Criminal Court and ended his life as United States Consul at Glasgow following Bret Harte. Next, Howells, who came, like the new incumbent, from New York and the *Nation,* to assist Fields, to be editor himself for a decade, assisted in turn by Hawthorne's son-in-law, George Parsons Lathrop. Miss Francis herself seemed to have been Aldrich's only aide, but Scudder, who, besides wielding the trident of the *Atlantic,* was literary adviser to the house, a copious producer of textbooks, juveniles, reviews, introductions, and biographies, read Latin and Greek half an hour before breakfast every day, wrote the editorial correspondence personally by hand, and ten pages or so of his Journal before going to bed, needed and had many. His included Mark Howe, a chiel among them taking notes for future admirable New England biographies; Frederic Lawrence Knowles, an old Middletown friend, who looked like Emerson, but whose

poetry was not quite so good; even, for a short time, Bliss
Carman.

In his *New England: Indian Summer,* remarkable for its
exquisite veracity in the resurrection of time past, Van Wyck
Brooks introduces some two hundred and thirty literary fig-
ures of that season of mists and mellow fruitfulness. Of these,
though it now seems incredible, I was personally acquainted
with one hundred and ninety-two. The proprietors of the
Atlantic were the publishers of all the so-called great New
England authors save Parkman, Louisa Alcott, and Emily
Dickinson of the later group, whose writings were marketed
by Little and Brown, good neighbors down on Washington
Street and later higher up the hill. The complete works of
Emerson, Thoreau, Longfellow, Holmes, Lowell, and Whit-
tier were sold in long sets, both through the trade and by
subscription, and turned over in myriad ways as textbooks for
the young. They were still the backbone of the business,
and gave the *Atlantic,* practically a house organ, a traditional
prestige that brought in admirable manuscripts, which grew
from chapter to chapter into good books — some of them,
like those of Fiske, Burroughs, John Muir, and Lafcadio
Hearn, providing more long sets.

A strayed reveller from New York was an odd note in the
New England autumn symphony, something like an unexpected accidental sharp. But the Park Street connection gave
him a certain social weight that he could hardly have attained
by his own indifferent efforts. Perhaps hostesses liked to
soften him in the hopes of selling their sonnets. The best
passport to superior literary society was an acquaintance with
the writings of Dante, then a name to conjure with in Boston
and Cambridge literary circles. So it had been since the day

reported by Howells, who had entered the study at Elmwood, chanting,

Io son cantava, io son dolce sirena,
Che i marinari in mezzo il mare dismago —

and Lowell, in hopeless admiration, had responded, O damn!

In 1902, the really 'great' New England authors, all save Aldrich, who was almost one, slept with their fathers in Mount Auburn, or Concord, or Amesbury, but one of the first impressions at Park Street was of the number of hale old men that came in, their youthfulness, their freedom from crotchets, their joy of life. Here was John T. Trowbridge, author of *Cudjo's Cave,* and *Darius Green and His Flying Machine,* ruddy as an apple, booming like a fog horn; Colonel Higginson, less ruddy than Trowbridge, but with a military set to his shoulders, recalling his command of a colored regiment, which he had recorded in the most virile of his writings; or Shaler, brilliant geologist, turned poet at eighty in a pentalogy of Elizabethan blank verse plays. He came in one day, looking, with pointed beard and high narrow brow, like Sir Walter Raleigh in person. He was in a glow, having walked the four miles from Cambridge. On Harvard Bridge, he had passed an aged Irishman, not making such good weather of it. As Shaler breezed by, he had shouted, 'Kin ye кape it up?' To which Shaler: 'You bet your sweet life I can kape it up!' Or Mr. Justice Holmes, hero of his father's *My Hunt After the Captain.* Age never staled his infinite variety. He was over ninety when, lunching with him one day at Beverly Farms, I was prompted to report: 'I heard a lady speak well of you the other day, Mr. Holmes.'

'A lady speak well of me!' and, rising on one leg, the other lifted with bent knee behind him, he blew a graceful kiss into the circumambient air. When it was revealed to him that the well-speaking lady was Willa Cather, whose work he admired, he was the more deeply pleased, and did it again in still handsomer style.

Nor were the old ladies of Boston less remarkable than the men. One night at dinner, Mrs. Jack Gardner, all in white, turned to me from the left and hurled: 'God only knows what Aristophanes has meant to me in my life.'

A gentle cross-examination revealed that this was perfectly true, and that it may even have had some reference to the conversation of the correct gentleman on her other side.

Best of all were the ladies of 148 Charles Street, where, in the long Victorian drawing room looking out over the Back Bay to the sunset — of how much of mellowness and charm — one found Mrs. Fields and her house mate, Miss Jewett, ready to giggle girlishly at any slightly malicious anecdote of the Boston great, or to expound their joint philosophy of the happy life, which consisted quite simply in taking short views. Mrs. Fields, faded, but of a still appealing beauty, carried, consciously and victoriously, the torch of an older tradition. Miss Jewett, in all her works and ways, was the living refutation of the proposition in *Expression in America,* that an artist cannot be a lady, or a lady an artist — if any refutation were needed after Jane Austen!

Charles Street, too, was a likely spot to encounter Mrs. Helen Bell, daughter of Rufus Choate, from Hog Island in the Essex Marshes, who, when the judge on the bench inquired, 'Mr. Choate, are you trying to show your contempt for this court?' replied, 'No, your Honor, I am trying to conceal it.' She was the sister of Joseph Choate, reputed the wittiest of American Ambassadors to the Court of St. James's.

Some of her whimsicalities are well known: to a friend going into the country, which she loathed, 'Kick a tree for me';
or, of that new invention the automobile: 'It will divide
mankind into two classes, the quick and the dead.' Her true
flavor is better conveyed in some items from the too brief
biography, by her friend Mrs. Drown:

'Cleopatra possessed her imagination. In talking once of
those "fields of the Cloth of Gold," where sacred and profane
history met, Herod's flirtation with Cleopatra was mentioned. She had never happened to hear of it, and exclaimed,
"What, *our* Herod! Why are we so calm about it?"

'Edward the Seventh was "Edward the Caresser."

'Of some handsome woman she said, "People speak of her
as a 'great still woman.' When I was growing up, we should
have called her dull."

'Of a woman who wanted to hold her hand, "Personally I
would rather hold the corner cabman's hand, it seems more
normal."

'The secret of her catholic taste was a real sympathy. As
you talked with her, you knew she was the most brilliant
woman in the world and you felt that you were a close
second.'

At seventy, her hair was still red-gold, her eyes twinkling,
her figure small, plump, and pleasing. She confided to her
biographer that when a young Mr. F. G. called on her in
Chestnut Street, to urge her to write her reminiscences, 'no
schoolgirl could have been more overcome.' Her caller was
overcome, too. A witty lady of his present entourage informs
him that a woman is only as old as she makes a man feel. If
that is true, Mrs. Bell was indeed a schoolgirl.

The *Atlantic* was becoming an international literary magazine, as well as a house organ for New England authors. In

my first months on Park Street, I had an experience that was described in the *Atlantic* in a passage of a slightly purplish tinge that now seems better suited to an end than to a beginning:

'On a memorable day a good many years ago a certain sub-editor, exploring the morning's mail, found his senses enthralled by a weird, sad, delicious odor. Perfumes in the mail were not unheard-of: violets there had been, and musk, and orange blossoms, and tobacco; and the sub-editor, with a fantasy appropriate to his station, even prided himself on his ability to close his eyes and pick out a California contribution by the unaided sense of smell. But never before had there been anything like this. Its chief essence was sandalwood, that was clear, but sandalwood so etherealized and mingled with I know not what of exotic scents that it gave to the imagination a provocative ghostly thrill indescribable. The basket of the Muses, hastily tumbled, disclosed a portentous envelope of straw color, with queer blue stamps in one corner, and queer unknown characters in another; yet queerest of all was the address in an odd orientalized hand, done with delicate, curiously curving strokes of the pen. Within, in a script still less Spencerian, these words met the sub-editor's excited eyes:

THE DREAM OF AKINOSUKE

By Lafcadio Hearn

' "In the district called Toichi of Yamato province, there used to live a goshi named Miyata Akinosuke"; and so on through some twenty pages, telling a mystical legend of Old Japan in a lovely and melodious English style.'

Lafcadio Hearn became important in my work. I corresponded with him, and, later, with his widow, Setsu Koizumi; fought battles with his detractors, in one instance barely avoiding physical violence; arranged for his *Life and Letters,* and introduced collections of his literary remains, feeling all the while that I was at last dealing with an authentic, if sub-calibre, genius. Every Christmas for several years, a case of sparkling Tan-san water, best of mixers, was delivered at my door from Japan.

After removal to the Brahmin slope of Park Street, I still revisited the Bohemian pastures that lay around the Library. The closest bond with the immediate past was continued com-merce with the stimulating artistic mind of Truman H. Bart-lett, of the Victoria round table, now forgotten, save by a diminishing rearguard of obsolescents who fell under his spell. His rough cottage house at Chocorua, complete with billiard table and unlimited beer, was the gathering place and asylum of a talented circle, including E. A. Robinson, William Vaughn Moody, and Daniel Gregory Mason.

Bartlett was truly, as Moody wrote Mason, 'a magnificent old goat.' Starting life as a marble-cutter in Vermont, his *bas-reliefs,* on tombstones, caught the eye of certain rich ama-teurs, who provided funds to take him to Paris. There he arrived, after a fructifying visit en route to Walt Whitman, bearing in his arms his passport to Parnassus, a replica in plaster of the Volk life mask of Lincoln. He tells of its effect:

'It is to Frenchmen that the credit of first seeing the true beauty of the life mask, of appreciating and describing it, is due. When, in 1877, I took a plaster copy to the oldest bronze founder in Paris, to get it cast in bronze, I put it down on a table side by side with a mask of the Abbé Lamennais. The first words of the founder were: "What a beautiful face!

Why, it's more beautiful and has more character than the Abbé's, and we think that is the handsomest one in France! What an extraordinary construction, and what fine forms it has." '

With the mask in bronze, he crashed the studios of Frémiet and Rodin. They admired it even more enthusiastically, and took its bearer into their circle devoted to *vin rouge,* French billiards, and intimate talk about art. Back home again, he taught these subjects at the Massachusetts Institute of Technology, together with the history, appreciation, and practice of sculpture; but, beyond a few portrait figures and busts, never himself produced.

In a vivid chapter of his *Music in My Time,* Mason quotes examples of Bartlett's startling gift of vision and phrase. He pointed one evening to the peaks of the Sandwich Range across Chocorua Lake, sharply silhouetted in the clear autumn air, and said, 'Look at the gravity of those mountains.' I find a letter from him written at Chocorua, concluding, 'It is peaceful here, — like a flageolet!'

His quality and the kernel of his own autobiography are in the concluding paragraph of his one remarkable book, *The Art Life of William Rimmer:*

'He felt art in all its varied phases, and touched, perhaps unconsciously, every one of its mighty chords.

'I say unconsciously; because I must believe, that had he really known their vast meaning, their resounding power, their majestic consolation, their imposing obligatory response, he would have entered into an extravagant exercise of them, despite all difficulties. For a man capable of so much to know, that, for reasons beyond his control, he cannot do his best, is one of the bitterest inflictions that helpless humanity is forced to endure.'

Happily, he lived to see his own dreams and ambitions completely fulfilled by his son Paul, whose magnificent Lafayette stands, or did stand when last heard from, in the fore court of the Louvre.

CHAPTER 8 ~

Shady Hill

IN HIS SECOND PARK STREET SPRING, Bartlett's beer and billiard refuge, with its view of the grave mountains, sheltered the first weeks of the sub-editor's marriage. It became the custom, first *à deux*, then with growing family expanded to *partie carrée*, to visit Chocorua each spring for the early fishing in a score of murmuring brooks and little rivers. Like the Great Carrying Place and the Lake, the hill and mountain country around Chocorua and Tamworth became part of the landscape background of my mind. In the autumn we settled in Cambridge on the short thoroughfare that leads from the Washington Elm to Brattle Street, so well described as not really a street but a state of mind; overhead lived the aged sister of James Russell Lowell's first wife.

First impressions of the University City were not gay. The creaking of board walks under the feet of the milkman awoke me regularly at four A.M. to wonder why I had ever left the quiet of New York. The large chilly frame houses, of a faded olive drab, seemed suitable containers for the society that Henry Adams had found a faculty meeting without business. A favorite evening's diversion was a social club which met at the house of its members in rotation. The host of the evening read a paper presenting his latest discoveries and conclusions in the field of his specialty. The men listened with frowning attention, supported by the prospect of refreshments to come, the women with that expression of eager, even breathless, interest which they can so readily and charmingly assume. When lecture gave place to liquor, all seemed to experience a certain relief.

These, however, were surface impressions, soon to be revised. In one of those olive drab houses I spent many rewarding hours. It stood on the eastern frontier of the town, a long two-story dwelling celebrated in the biographical literature of two continents as Shady Hill. It was reached by an avenue between elms, paralleled by another board walk winding up an easy hill through some five or six acres of grassy grounds. In it lived Charles Eliot Norton.

The letters, reminiscences and formal writings of Norton's former students and academic colleagues are full of words like 'preciosity,' and 'fastidiousness,' conveying a judgment neatly summarized by Van Wyck Brooks: 'Like his sympathies, his imagination was imperfectly developed. There had always been something wrong with a standard that led to this denial of life, a denial that was sterile and complacent.'

Yet in the letters written to him by Carlyle, Ruskin, Edward Fitzgerald, Sir Leslie Stephen, or Lowell, and in Norton's to them and a score of others, one finds a sympathy and a responsive fire of imagination that are the stuff of friendship that, so far from being its denial, is the very breath of life.

Perhaps imperfect sympathy in those around him drove him to an overemphasis of his own position that hardened to a pose. Little of that was left in the days of his serene retirement. In 1898, when Norton had opposed the Spanish

War, John Jay Chapman had written of him as 'a man born blind with the religion of pictures, a deaf man worshipping music, a man devoid of sensuous experience erecting altars to the Aesthetic'; a characteristic tone that led William James to write him, on another occasion, that a good description of his style was to be found in the words of a certain witness in a poisoning case who, when asked what the corpse looked like, replied: 'Pleasant-like and foaming at the mouth.'

But later, in *Memories and Milestones,* Chapman wrote of Norton:

'At the age of eighty he was plainly nothing else than a darling old saint, with a few sophistical hobbies, which if you went to see him he drew from his cabinet and showed you with glee — old philosophical gimcracks. These things you perceived at once to be of no importance. The man himself was everything.'

Norton was well on for eighty when I first made the ascent of Shady Hill, was smilingly received, given a seat by the fire and a very dry panetela cigar, and advised about the biography of Lowell I had been asked to undertake for the American Men of Letters Series. I fell into the habit of stopping at Shady Hill at ten-thirty each Wednesday morning for talk about Lowell, and past and current literature.

As a reviewer of opus number four was to point out, it took a certain amount of courage in a young man from New York, writing on Lowell in Cambridge in 1904, to be 'the first to report the verdict of posterity.' I never should have dared the adventure had I not found that Norton, Lowell's lifelong friend, his literary executor, and the editor of his letters, shared both my enthusiasms and my reservations. The darling old saint was no mere praiser of time past; few men of a not inconsiderable literary acquaintance, even wish-thinking publishers, have been more eager to find new talent, few have been more catholic in its recognition.

In the nineties, he gave Kipling his first welcome, both to Cambridge and to the upper circle of British poets, a judgment that has just been confirmed half a century later by T. S. Eliot, subtlest of living critics. It has been discovered that at the age of twenty-seven, in 1855, he was the author of an unsigned review in *Putnam's Magazine* of the first edition of Whitman's *Leaves of Grass,* one of the two or three that felt its quality. There were passages in the poems that sounded strange to Andrews Norton's son, who at the age of two had sat on the knee of Wordsworth. He saw in it a combination of 'the characteristics of a Concord philosopher with those of a New York Fireman,' and in his heart seemed rather to relish both. He described it as 'this gross yet elevated, this superficial yet profound, this preposterous yet somehow fascinating book.' He procured a copy for Lowell, who was in Dresden, and wrote him eagerly about it. By return mail, without waiting to receive the book and read it, Lowell lectured him at length and roundly for presuming to like it. 'No, no, the kind of thing you describe won't do!'

Norton saw the writings of his friend Lowell from the point of view of the present rather than the past century. He poured out recollections and provided manuscript materials. At one point there was a slight divergence of view. After reading proofs of the first chapters, Norton wrote:

'It might perhaps be well to say something in your account of Lowell's early manhood of what in a general way may be called the influence of the change wrought by the progress of democratic conditions on social relations. Lowell's family belonged to the Brahmin caste alike by inheritance and culture. But Lowell separated himself from this caste, to which

by taste and culture he belonged, not only by his abolition-
ism but by his choice of friends and by his marriage. Hence
arose a division and conflict in his interior as well as his ex-
terior life, with results which were not happy for his natural
development.'

I was, I am afraid, more interested in the democratic social
sympathies of Hosea Biglow than in the Brahmin background
of his creator, and said so in the new paragraph. As for that
'interior conflict,' I regret now that I did not print the self-
epitaph found among the manuscript odds and ends.

> Here lies that part of J. R. L.
> That hindered him from doing well.

Nevertheless, when the book was published, Norton was
content with it and wrote, 'I believe, as well as hope, that
your book will be accepted as the "standard" account of him
and his work.' Some reviewers agreed; some dismissed the
author as an upstart; several rebuked him for the pleasure
he still took in putting the sixteen-pound word. My good
friend Harry Boynton complained in the *New York Times,*
'He chooses to send us to the dictionary rather than deprive
his own initiated palate of some subtle flavor of meaning.'
I plead guilty, but can think of many less agreeable and
profitable domestic trips than that to the Dictionary. It was
reassuring when Louise Imogen Guiney, to whom Lionel
Johnson on his bed of death said, 'Louise, when I am gone
you will be the colon's only friend,' wrote, 'Dearest of Sirs:
Your style is apples, crisp and juicy.'

The mornings at Shady Hill continued even after the affair
of Lowell was over. In one of his early letters to Woodberry,
Norton had written, 'The frequency of the expression of

affection is a very important thing in human life.' If he liked you he made you feel it, in his smiling welcomes and delaying farewells, in the expressions with which his beautifully written, deliberately phrased letters concluded. He seemed to have a special benevolence for strangers from without the Harvard gates, literary aspirants from Maine or the Middle West, strayed revellers from New York. On the evening of his last valediction, Miss Jewett wrote to Howells:

'I saw you today at the Appleton Chapel and I felt as one sometimes feels at the sight of an old friend — a new spring coming from a deeper place in the hillside of life, of attachment and affection. And I thought that you in your friendship and I in mine with dear Mr. Norton know some things together and hold them with dear love and gratitude for our very own, that many of the old Cambridge neighbors and cousins of varying degrees could never know. Maine and Ohio had not given you and me certain things that his kind hold waiting.'

To visit him was rather like a symposium with Plato, particularly if an opportunity arose for a sly dig at Aristotle. The Aristotelian who chiefly provoked him was President Charles W. Eliot. For a time I had occasion to see both rather frequently, and found it amusing to quote the one to the other on some current question or event. The response from each was always identical: 'Oh, my cousin Charles,' in a tone indicating a voluntary but temporary suspension of disbelief.

The small dinner parties at Shady Hill were memorable events. I remember one at which the other guests were Howells, who had not forgotten Dansville, and Norton's brother-in-law, Arthur Sedgwick, from Stockbridge. The talk turned on American humor and it was agreed that each should tell whatever anecdote seemed to him the best example of it.

Norton began with a very good one about a Yankee sailor, his shipmate when as a young man he had served as supercargo on an East India Clipper. Mr. Sedgwick told an equally good one from the Berkshire Hills.

I offered a rather less good one heard in New York, illustrating the pervasive American humor of phrase. A stout landlady of Shelburne, New Hampshire, had been so busy with boarders that she said to one of them, Paul Elmer More for the record:

'I ain't set my heft all summer!'

Last came Howells:

'Once upon a time, there was a horse trade between a farmer and a broker. After a prolonged dicker, the broker said,

' "What is the rock-bottom price you will take for the horse?"

' "One thousand dollars," said the farmer.

' "I'll give you a hundred," said the broker, to which the farmer:

' "It's a hell of a discount, but I'll take it." '

All laughed, not very heartily.

'Wait,' said Howells, holding up his hand. 'We haven't reached the American humor yet. As the broker was driving off with the horse, he pulled up. "Whoa, I wish you'd tell me why you asked me a thousand dollars for this horse when you were willing to take a hundred?"

' "Wal," said the farmer, "I kind of thought maybe you might want a thousand-dollar hoss." '

Where is that party now? Like Hans Breitman's, its laughter, save for this last echo, lost in *die Ewigkeit!* Norton faded out of a world in which the internal combustion engine was already firmly established, and died in the autumn of 1908, at the age of eighty-one. It was deeply moving to learn that, in the last week of his life, his daughters had read to him his affectionate admirer's *Life of Aldrich,* that it gave him pleasure.

CHAPTER 9

Sea-change

BEFORE THE ACTUAL WRITING of the Lowell was completed, a project of long standing had been carried out — to spend a month at Taormina under the sky-filling slope of Mount Etna, by the curving shore beloved of both Theocritus and Woodberry. On the coldest night of a cold winter, the water pipes frozen in the cabins, we sailed from Boston for the Mediterranean on the *Romanic.*

There is more of history, human interest, even spice in Homer's famous catalogue of ships than those who have been permitted to by-pass it in school can imagine. If only for my own nostalgic pleasure, I should like to record a catalogue of the ships in which I have made nearly half a hundred North Atlantic crossings taking, all told, more than fifty-two weeks — a year of life on the high seas.

First, then, the *Romanic,* from which I saw the loveliest of foreign landfalls, Pico in the Azores rising from the morning sea. Then a procession of Boston-Queenstown-Liverpool White Star boats and Cunarders, on which I shuttled back and forth, on some twice, on one three times: *Cymric, Cedric, Canopic, Adriatic, Baltic, Britannic, Scythia, Laconia, Franconia, Tuscania, Samaria.* I can recall their individual smells and motions, and the pleasant companions of each voyage. Then the bigger, faster, New York boats, sailing for or from Cherbourg, Southampton, Fishguard, Plymouth — the *Lusitania, Aquitania, Carmania, Queen Mary, Olympic, Homeric, Majestic*. I had engaged passage on the *Titanic* for her first and last voyage, but finished my work earlier than expected and came home on the *Mauretania* just ahead, seeing ice in the exact latitude and longitude where the *Titanic* sank.

Every voyage made some history of its own. On the *Lusitania* in 1908, a member of a syndicate of three, I took in a third of the auction pool every day of a record four-day and nineteen-hour passage from Daunt's Rock to Sandy Hook. On landing I bought my own first internal combustion engine, mounted in a Buick 'surrey,' and loved it for myself, but distrusted it for the world. The great toe, hitherto unregarded among the nobler members of the body, had become master of brake and throttle and lord of life and death.

On one trip the *Aquitania* rolled for three days through an arc of more than thirty degrees, breaking, so it was stated by the barber, three thousand pounds' worth of crockery and furniture and sending seventy first-cabin passengers to the surgeon to be treated for contusions, abrasions, fractures, and sprains. One night the Atlantic Ocean smashed a ventilator cover, entered my cabin, and swashed around to the depth of more than a foot. Standing one day on the forward deck, admiring the roll, I gave instructive information concerning the habits of porpoises and other nautical matters to a stranger, who later introduced himself as Sir Ernest Shackleton, the Antarctic explorer!

Finally, there were the American, French, and Dutch boats; the *Finland*, from whose boat deck, off Fastnet in January,

1917, a German submarine was seen to sink a Russian barque, the *Old North State,* the *Minnewaska,* the *Leviathan,* the *Paris,* on which you couldn't breathe fresh air even on deck but only the pervasive essences of Ed. Pinaud; the *Rotterdam,* of a specially happy memory; and the *New Amsterdam,* on which I arrived in New York Harbor from Brest in March, 1919, in the early days of near-beer, adding a mite to the roar arising from three thousand thirsty throats:

> How dry I am, how dry I am,
> God only knows how dry I am.

Taormina proved to be even lovelier and more richly saturated with historic association than expected. I found there a Park Street author, Mary Johnston, recuperating from the production of *Lewis Rand,* and a little group was formed which read Theocritus with his scenes before their eyes. I have the slim blue volume still, a Sicilian daisy pressed between its leaves. For *uno cinquanta* I purchased a pipe from a shepherd, and played it with a virtuosity that led an aged crone driving a donkey up a steep and stony path to thrust her head over the wall, crack a leathery smile and say: 'The signore plays the best of any *forestiere* that ever came to Sicily.'

From that the signore dates a liking for the Italian people that has survived even the strutting of their German-silver Caesar.

At Taormina I had my only conversation with an Imperial Majesty. A few days after we had settled ourselves comfortably in the Casa Timeo, Kaiser Wilhelm II arrived to see the sights so warmly recommended by the great Goethe. The next morning, I was doing the hundred steps on the terrace that looks out over the ruins of the Greek theatre to the sixty-mile shore line to Syracuse, margining the wine-dark sea, the magnificent pictorial setting of five major conquests.[1] Suddenly, as I turned smartly on the heel, I came face to face with the Emperor doing the same. I saluted. The Emperor gave me a glance whose bright-eyed, searching quality I vividly remember, and said, with an Oxford cadence, 'A magnificent view.'

I agreed, and ventured to add, 'And historic, Sir.'

The sabre-rattler accepted the addition with a smile. Later in the day, the padrone of the Casa requested us to move out of our quarters to make room for the imperial chamberlain, and I transferred Theocritus and shepherd's pipe to the Castellamare, down the hill nearer the purple waves.

In Naples, three weeks later I saw his Imperial Majesty attended by a squad of big, blond-bearded, terrifically Nordic sailors from a battleship in the harbor, driving along the Via Santa Lucia through a silent, rather sullen Latin crowd. It was very different the following week in Rome, when Emile Loubet, President of the French Republic, came down from Paris to pay a visit of state. The streets were placarded with posters reminding the populace that French and Italians were both descended from Julius Caesar, that they were all Free Masons, exhorting them to throw no bombs. They didn't, and the pale, black-bearded President rode in triumph, and a deluge of confetti, through miles of shouting Roman citizens.

After reading the local press and stray copies of the *London Times* and *Manchester Guardian,* I took in what it was all about. The new Anglo-French *entente* was being cooked

---

[1] As I deal with the proofs of this page the United Nations have made it six.

up in London, it was hoped that Italy might be friendly to it; and Germany and Austria were worried about their reluctant partner's attitude toward the Triple Alliance, which was soon coming up for renewal. It was renewed, but with no diminution of the distrust and dislike prevailing between the contracting parties.

Back in Cambridge, I battled for more than a year with the recrudescences of a Roman fever, contracted while escorting Mary Johnston, by auto, across the mosquito-infested campagna to hear the nightingale sing in the ruins of the villa where the Emperor Hadrian and John Keats had listened to that selfsame song. The daily trip to Park Street by surface trolley began to pall. After two years in the shade of the Washington Elm, and another on a short avenue named after the Baroness Riedesel, who knew the Lake and the Great Carrying Place only too well, it was decided to move into Boston, that I might walk to work across the Common, swinging my stick. A small, tall house was bought on one of the wobbly streets that run along the westerly slope of Beacon Hill.

For a time, life flowed smoothly, its current broadening. I joined a club devoted to literature and art and was thrilled to find that Francis Parkman had been its first president. As the New England Indian Summer faded, writers, painters, and musicians became less numerous than editors, publishers, lawyers, and doctors. Art and literature shrank a little in importance. Conversation concerning them was replaced in part by billiards, bridge, backgammon, dominoes, and as knowledgable fishing talk as is to be found anywhere outside of the Flyfishers Club in Piccadilly. Again today it shelters historical novelists and historians after the first president's own heart; men who get around and write with style — their eye on the object — Bruce Lancaster, Walter Edmonds, Samuel Eliot Morison.

But the barometer was set for change.

The motor car had not yet made country life a joy in widest commonalty spread; weekend visits to friends in the near-by country were more momentous than they are today. Nothing brought more joy to West Cedar Street than an invitation from Mrs. Fields to Thunderbolt Hill in Manchester-by-the-Sea. There one enjoyed the best of literary conversation and the acme of refined comfort, so refined, indeed, that in the guest chambers all articles of domestic china possessing lids were provided with knitted sound-dampeners. The lid, if removed for any purpose, could be restored to its base in nothing less than a luscious silence. To my fantastic imagination these, although not suitable to be engraved on its cover, always seemed the perfect symbols of the *Atlantic Monthly*. I tried to imagine what would happen if the dampener were removed. I was soon to find out.

In 1906, on the eve of the semi-centennial of the *Atlantic's* birth, B. P. took a sabbatical half-year off, and sailed for Europe, leaving the magazine to the care of a proud subeditor. The first order of business was to find an attractive serial novel for the coming anniversary year. May Sinclair's *The Divine Fire* had been the outstanding fictional success of the previous year in both England and America. It seemed a sound idea to apply for the serial rights of her new book, but when the manuscript of *The Helpmate* arrived at Park Street, it presented a problem. It was a realistic, powerful, provocative story of an unsatisfactory marriage. While it did not seem likely to lead anyone astray from the straight and narrow path, it was slightly lacking in conventional reticence. It opened with a conversation in bed between husband and wife. I knew I was dealing with dynamite, but, remembering the belated regret of the firm at having declined the first English translation of *Anna Karenina* on grounds of impropriety, decided, like Richard Ferris, to take a chance. I removed the dampener from the *Atlantic's* lid and accepted it.

The result was cataclysmic. The Watch and Ward Society never became excited about it, but, after the first instalment appeared in an autumn number, subscriptions were cancelled by the score, chiefly from Boston. In the end, on balance, the magazine enjoyed the largest increase in circulation it had had in any one year up to that time. What B. P. really felt in his heart about *The Helpmate*, I have never found out, but, as he must have spent most of his time for months after his return writing patient letters to outraged subscribers, it is possible that he did not care greatly for it. There was a conference at which it was decided that my talent for shocking the public was wasted on the *Atlantic*, and I was transferred to the book end of the business as its editorial adviser.

At first, it was almost like the happy old free-shooter days. I was relieved of routine, and was asked to undertake the authorized biography of Thomas Bailey Aldrich, then recently deceased. The wise and understanding head of the firm, George H. Mifflin, thought it well that before getting deeply into that, and before my desk was buried under the complicated trouble every publisher knows, I should make a voyage to England, meet authors, publishers and agents, and generally acquire an 'international point of view.' When this proposition was put to me, I replied without hesitation, like the Viziers to their Sultans in *Arabian Nights*, '*j'écoute et j'obéis,'* and sailed forthwith on the *Cymric* for the first of over a score of visits to the British Isles. Not counting the ocean passages, they made up in the aggregate more than two of my best and busiest years.

CHAPTER 10

England

I SEE HER FROM THE SEA almost in the round: her busy ports, Liverpool, Bristol, Fishguard, Falmouth, Plymouth, Southampton, Portsmouth, Newhaven, Folkestone, Dover, Tilbury; the landfalls and thoroughfares between, the Scilly Isles, the Lizard, Sheerness; St. George's Channel, the Straits of Dover, the Mull of Kintyre. I see the hills tramped over under misty suns and un-wetting rains, Exmoor, Dartmoor, the Cotswolds, the Downs, the Moors of Yorkshire; the rivers I fished, the Tay with John Buchan, the Wye with Rafael Sabatini, the Tees, with Harry Morritt of Rokeby; the Barle, the Exe, the Coln, the Dart, the Evenlode, the Windrush; highlands of Scotland and water meadows of Hampshire. I walk the murky streets of London and Liverpool, Glasgow and Edinburgh, the gardens and lawns of Oxford and Cambridge, the crescents and quadrants of Bath. I revisit hospitable castles and country houses, and friendly thatched cottages; palace hotels, country inns, clubs and pubs and cabman's shelters; I loiter in cathedrals and parish churches, crypts and graveyards, haunts of ancient peace.

How ancient, how peaceful and how haunting the mortuary inscription I copied from the floor of the Early-Norman church at Burford on the Windrush!

> In this grave together lie
> Grey age, green youth, white infancie.
> They that lived and loved the ither,
> Shall die and lie and sleep togither.

There are talking pictures, too.

I remember conversations with sailors, soldiers, porters, hawkers, railway guards, police constables, detectives from Scotland Yard, cab-drivers, taxi-drivers, engine-drivers, valets, grooms, butlers, gillies, a fishing duke, water bailiffs, game-keepers, shopkeepers, innkeepers, schoolboys, university boys, tutors, dons, professors, regius professors, parsons, wardens, deans, bishops, painters, publishers, authors, a couple of poets laureate, actors, agents, editors, scientists, solicitors, barristers, King's counsel, judges, doctors, surgeons, bookmakers, bankers, beggars, brokers, baronets, members of Parliament, peers of the realm, cabinet ministers, ambassadors, agitators, admirals, generals, governor-generals, secretaries of state for foreign affairs, under-secretaries *de toute espèce,* prime ministers, labor leaders, a viceroy, country gentlemen, gentlemen jockeys, travellers, explorers and adventurers; together with the ladies of most of them, and others.

I cannot recall meeting any of the 'horse-riding snobs,' denounced by the author of *The American Tragedy.* I found them a friendly, free-spoken race, with no nonsense about them, recalling Montesquieu's affirmation, 'No people have true common sense but those who are born in England.' They wore comfortable clothes. It has been said the Frenchman invented the ruffle, the Englishman invented the shirt. If, through their history, they have never known when they were beaten, neither have they seemed to me, however blue their noses, to know when they were cold, or even when they were unhappy. If the French offered cakes and wine, the English served beef and beer. Yet their poets take us closer than those of any other nation to the very brink of the night and the morning, to faëry lands forlorn. What other dictionary of national biography is so rich in varied talent, or, from a thousand years of history and thirty thousand names from Abbadie to Zuylestein, brings together so many men one would like to have known?

On the advice of Royal Cortissoz, I avoided the larger London hotels and settled in Garland's at the top of the *cul de sac* of Suffolk Street, off Pall Mall. It was an Early-Victorian hostelry, beloved of the upper clergy, half-pay colonels and their womenfolk. It had been the residence of Whistler for many years and the London headquarters of Anthony Trollope. I frequented it for a third of a century, usually in the Trollope suite, until the march of progress put in a public lounge and cocktail bar. In the old days it had a chilly 'Coffee Room,' but the regulars ate, and solidly, in their own apartments, by their fires of cannel coal. Its three stories were pierced by an anti-aircraft shell in the Old War, and it has been, one hears, completely demolished in this.

In a busy month I met most of the publishers, all the literary agents and many of the authors of London. I was disconcerted to find that I was considered a child of the literary loins of Walter Pater.

Of the publishers there were three in particular with whom as the years went by I was to have many and intimate dealings. Scott's old publishers, Constable and Company, then under the managing directorship in alternate years of Otto Kyllman and George Meredith's son William, later joined by Michael Sadleir, author-publisher, who after leaving Balliol, not ill-equipped with its effortless superiority, cut his publishing teeth in an office commanding the Old Granary Burying Ground in Boston; Grant Richards, epicure in authorship as in gastronomy; and William Heineman, distinguished in the trade for his single-minded devotion to the best in literature. For him, profits seemed never an end in themselves, but only an agreeable by-product of publishing good writing.

Heineman had a queer streak of sentiment, of *morbidezza* in the full Italian sense, so different from mere morbidity. On the mantel of his library in Lower Belgrade Street rested a smallish human skull, lined with silver. Only after his death did I learn its story. During one of his visits to Florence, a young girl, unknown and never identified, had drowned herself in the Arno. The incident held Heineman's imagination in thrall. He had secured the skull from the authorities and lived with it under his eye for the rest of his life. Although he was dark and bald, his cable address was 'Sunlocks.'

From that first British visit I remember, too, tall, scholarly-looking Reginald Smith, head of Smith Elder, son-in-law and successor to George Smith, who converted the handsome profits from the sale of the works of the Brontës, Darwin, Trollope, Browning, and Thackeray, plus those of the Apollinaris Spring, of which he was proprietor, into the great project of the biographical dictionary. Reginald Smith entertained his young American visitor by carefully removing all the contents of his trousers pockets and turning them completely inside out. That, he explained, was the manner in which Thackeray always entered the office of his publisher. When he took me across the hall to be introduced to the editor of the *Cornhill,* Leonard Huxley, I felt that these were the seats of the sons of the mighty.

Of the authors, the largest single round-up was one day at a lunch at the House of Lords given by Edmund Gosse, who had just become its librarian and complained alliteratively that his chief occupation was pointing quill pens for peers. Other guests were Lord Carlisle, a hawk-faced Italianate English-lishman like those who brought coloratura into Elizabethan literature; Barrie, whose tongue was silent but whose eyes reflected every shade of the conversation; Alfred Noyes, whose youthful figure set off the products of Savile Row to perfection; and the woolly-bearded poet, Sturge Moore. As Moore entered late, Gosse, a naughty host, whispered in my ear, 'A sheep in sheep's clothing.' But as the talk rose on the tide of the House's admirable cellar, the sheep proved the life of the party.

I had a first look at Oxford, guided by Louise Guiney, who knew what old worthy lay under every mossy stone, and understood both Pater and Glanvill better. I weekended at Winchelsea, where Ford Madox Hueffer, later Ford, free-holder of the Cinque Ports, who could wear his hat in the presence of the King, was advising both Conrad and Gals-worthy in their early efforts. There I heard talk of a dif-ferent flavor from any I had known in Boston and Cam-bridge. We drove over the marshes to Rye to pay respects to Henry James, but when the large white Georgian door opened inward from the village street a dour housekeeper, Mrs. Bathsheba Paddington, informed us: 'He isn't home. I sent him away for my spring cleaning, and I'll not have him back till it's entirely transacted.' This was a disappoint-ment. I had just been reading proof of an *Atlantic* article by Mr. James and was eager to inquire why the only author's corrections had been the removal of several adverbs from their natural to exhibitionist positions.

From the immediate professional point of view, my only accomplishment was bringing back Havelock Ellis's manuscript *The Soul of Spain*. I had penetrated to a cluttered hideout in the remotest corner of Camberwell and been charmed by the high eager voice that issued from the patriarchal beard adorning without concealing a thin and sensitive countenance.

On the last day in London, I was invited to take tea with Mr. George Bernard Shaw in his chambers in the Adelphi. Tea turned out to consist chiefly of buttermilk. Inspired by its fumes and by the sight of several tin whistles lying on a library table, I ventured to propose an amoebean contest. When Mrs. Shaw, led, no doubt, by sentiments of hospitality, awarded the guest the palm for piping, G. B. S. obviously conceived a low opinion of my brains and character which, on several future meetings, he took no pains to conceal.

Our last and roughest encounter was at dinner at the Joe Pennells', also in the Adelphi, just before the Old War. From behind a tall glass of milk that loomed palely above the glasses of the rest of the company, showing the dark ruby of a very special Burgundy, G. B. S., with eloquence and wit, denounced the United States, their population, and all their works, past, present, and future. When a question from Elizabeth Pennell discovered that the speaker had never visited the States, I ventured to remark as delicately as possible that the Shavian attack had a flavor of the closed mind, and suggested that the attacker spend three months in America, look us over and put his observations and conclusions into a book. I undertook to supply a sufficient advance against the author's royalties, known to be high, to cover all expenses.

At this Shaw, his Mephistophelian countenance at its most sardonic, shouted back: 'I wouldn't go to America for a million a minute; which I understand to be your favorite expression!'

There is some evidence that he thinks a little better of us now.

An hour later, I had the second shock of a seismic evening. As I walked along the Strand with small, demure, Miss May Sinclair, escorting her home by tube to Hampstead, a plump bare arm slid under mine from behind and a Bacchic fragrance breathed in my ear, 'Come 'ome with me, darlin', instead!'

For the acquisition of the international point of view, the high point of the trip was reached, not in London, but in Paris, where for a week I visited Paul Bartlett.

The dreams of life and art old Truman had entertained beside his marble quarry in Vermont had come to their aureate realization in Paul. Everything about him was rosy or golden, his glowing flesh, his shining hair and beard and mustache fiercely curling under an eagle's nose and smiling blue-eyed gaze, the scarlet button of a Commandeur of the Legion of Honor in his coat. His lovely colored bronzes, cast *à cire perdue,* were already established as something new and important in the sculpture of the West. His Columbus and his Michelangelo had been recognized as authentic masterpieces, and the first plaster model of his Lafayette, paid for by the dimes of a million American school-children, was in its place in front of the Louvre. As one strolled with him on the *Boule Miche*, it was 'Ah, cher maître, cher maître!' all along the way.

More than thirty of the forty years of his life had been spent in France; he spoke English with a lisping French accent, and, for the *mot* truly *juste,* always turned to his foster tongue. This lent a stimulating cosmopolitan flavor to his copious talk about the aims and methods of his art.

One night we sat over our red wine till long past midnight, discussing the physiognomy, character, and historical significance of Lafayette. Back in the cavernous studio, somewhere around two A.M., Bartlett turned on all the lights, removed the protecting cloths from a full-sized Lafayette in clay, walked around it and around for so long as it takes to smoke a Maryland; then climbed a ladder, rolled up his sleeves from two muscular rosy arms covered with golden down, and worked for perhaps an hour.

By a complicated piece of engineering he elevated the lifted sword to the limit of elevation, he slightly widened the parting of the lips, and he noticeably increased the slope of the receding brow. For the first time I comprehended what creative revision can accomplish in other arts than literature. Bartlett had given to his massive sticky material that final blithe suggestion of the young idealist-adventurer, not knowing quite where he is going, but very definitely on his way, that gives it convincing reality and lively charm.

> If but the will be firmly bent,
> No stuff resists the mind's intent.

A few months after that ambrosial evening I was walking along the back of the Capitol in Washington with Congressman S. W. McCall. Pointing to the blank pediment of the House wing, McCall said: 'That ought to have statuary on it.' I agreed and mentioned the name of a good man to put it there. Hardly was I back in Boston before a letter came from McCall, asking for further information. The National Sculpture Society was invited to make nominations. They provided a list of ten, with Paul Bartlett's name at the top.

Probably few of the visitors to the Capitol, not many of the men who make speeches under its dome, ever give a glance, still less a thought, to the lovely rhythmical composition that embellishes the pediment of the back entrance to the House. It represents Democracy Protecting the Arts of Peace. In the centre sits the generous figure of Democracy, a woman nobly planned. On the left are seen a Steelmaker, a Printer, a Weaver, a Fisherman; on the right, a Reaper, a Farmer with his Ox, a Housewife, and, down in the narrowing corner, complete with ram, what is described in official handbooks as a cherub, but which looks uncommonly like Dan Cupid, whatever he may be up to in that *galère*.

CHAPTER 11 ～

Enamoured
architect of airy rhyme

FROM MY FIRST DAYS at Park Street, I had seen a good deal of one of its earlier editors; as I thought, and still think, one of New England's finest poets. Hardly a week went by that Thomas Bailey Aldrich, blond, erect, and ruddy, seeming, at seventy, as immortal as a lyric, did not appear in the editorial offices on the third floor of Number Four, shouting his slogan, 'God, and my copyrights!' He found there an eager listener to stories of the *Atlantic's* blameless past, and criticism of the purity of its English in the present. As time went on, that willing ear came to be in occasional demand within the marble portals of 59 Mount Vernon Street, at the farm in Ponkapog, and on the wide, after-deck of the *Bethulia,* probably the only steam yacht of its size ever owned by a poet of his rank. The food and drink were good, the cigars and talk still better; with always a touch of poetry and impish humor. Aldrich was a lover of life; little Tom Bailey of Portsmouth, the bad boy who was still not such a very bad boy, lived on in him, and his sudden death was poignant like a boy's. It was as if a thrush had forsaken its familiar tree.

The *Life of Aldrich,* opus number five, the last that I was to undertake for more than thirty years, was less toil than pleasure. I collected a small safe full of letters, interviewed Aldrich's friends at home and abroad, and, standing aside as much as possible, let the poet tell his own story of what was, save for one great sorrow, a singularly happy life. For prose, I didn't put the stories and novels quite as high as the obituaries did, but thought *The Story of a Bad Boy* an authentic small 'classic.' Now, after seventy-five years and in the public domain, it still sells in substantial volume, in a dozen different editions, and can be read in half a dozen languages other than English. That from a publisher's point of view is the way a classic acts.

Of the poems I see I said:

'The most vitally characteristic, and we may believe the most enduring poems of Aldrich, the poems in which we have at once his genius in its purest intensity, and his art in its most nice perfection, are what we may call the anthology poems, like Nocturne, Palabras Carinosas, Two Songs from the Persian, Forever and a Day, and still more importantly, that series of tiny pieces of which no other American poet could conceivably have written a single one: Snowflake, Apparitions, Knowledge, An Untimely Thought, Destiny, Identity, Nameless Pain, A Winter Piece, Seeming Defeat, Rencontre, One White Rose, Prescience, Like Crusoe, Walking by the Lonely Strand, A Mood, Memory, Necromancy, Lost Art, I'll Not Confer with Sorrow, Pillared Arch and Sculptured Tower, Imogen — their very titles are poems.

'He immortalized the moment's exquisite pang of memory or joy or foreboding, not in shadowy, but in crystalline verse. Impulses the most romantic in the world he guided by an instinct that was purely classic in its inspired poise. His most characteristic work is that in which the terse polish of an epigram but makes memorable the *frisson*, the haunting, heart-searching thrill of the sudden thought.'

Well, that is the way it seems to have worked out. The pieces listed will be found fresh and firm today, and — a fair test — they have been, during the present century, more in demand from anthologists than any group of similar extent by any other New England poet. In the drawers of the cabinet at his publishers' that contains the card catalogue of 'Permissions Granted,' the Lowell cards, if tightly squeezed, occupy five-sixteenths of an inch, with only an entry or two or three to a card. The Aldrich cards, most of them fully covered with itemized permissions, squeezed just as tightly, consume a space of one full inch, and the five-sixteenths over.

Not long after the publication of the book, I received a letter from Woodberry, who had known Aldrich longer and more intimately than its author had. It adds something warming and real to the record of both poets:

'I am sorry that I knew nothing of the facts of his last years; being myself then in great vexation of my own at first, and afterwards out of the country and with a great sense of abandonment in my heart that I need not dwell on; I *had* to be alone those days, but I have that regret now that a man may have when an accident has taken place and he was not near and could neither help nor know. So in many ways for which you are nowise responsible there was much sadness in the book for me.

'What pleases me most is the cleverness and constancy of the literary flame in him from a boy. It is full of the old feeling that made Drake press his proofs to his cheek with a caress — there is that boyish first love in it, and, I was going to say, idolatry. He had it — the true love of letters — nothing else was much but phases of mortality to him — the wit, the diner-out, society, what-not. That and his home made up his life. He was, I think, a more home-hearted person, and a cleaver to his friends who were not great or literary at all, than appears in the book; but it is a difficult thing to give in a book. He could worry about people, and take thought for them, more than you show. He was, I think, generous, in the sense of giving his spirit to others, thinking of them, taking pains for them, doing things for them — little things, no doubt, but full of sympathy and affection and warm good will. You have shown him in his literary circle, when he was self-conscious and "alert" as you say: — he was never "alert" with me, that is when we were alone, but he was always alive — very simply and very humbly alive, not thinking at all about it.

'I feel I am writing too much; but I must say that though that side was not the world's part in him, and the world has no right to know more than his public life — still that was very genuine in him, and his literary friends did not recognize or know much about it (I think); he was a very different person from what New Yorkers thought, and of his Boston friends (the older, I mean), I fancy that only Lowell took to him completely — Lowell had that same good stuff in him; to them he was a New York *émigré*, "a brand plucked from the burning." His position, whether in New York or Boston, was never quite a true one: he was not a bird of either feather; but there was a quality about him that went into his daily life and never went into his books.'

There was indeed more of the man than was ever fully expressed in his writing. If word could be got to him where he sits in Elysium at the edge of the circle of Catullus and Herrick, with Dobson and Praed and old poet-friends from

New York and Cambridge, nothing would give him more pleasure, not even a report of the continuing sales of *The Story of a Bad Boy*, than the news that in 1942, on the West Coast, three thousand miles from Tom Bailey's Portsmouth, a ten-thousand-ton Liberty ship was launched and christened — with champagne — the *Thomas Bailey Aldrich*.

CHAPTER 12

New direction

DURING THE EIGHT YEARS of the reign of Theodore Roosevelt, I was finding pleasure and satisfaction in putting words together on paper, composing them, even in a book review, with a certain fury and correcting them with phlegm. I had painted the image of my thoughts in some hundreds of *Nation* articles, a score of literary papers in the *Atlantic,* the *Outlook,* the *Century, Scribner's,* and in four volumes of biography. After the publication of *Aldrich,* writing days ended abruptly. Save for a Preface or two, a fishing piece, and an article in the *Dictionary of American Biography,* my literary compositions for a third of a century consisted of quarterly reports to directors and stockholders, and some hundred thousand letters to authors concerning fifty thousand manuscripts, of which perhaps three thousand became published books. In the carefree days at the Lake I had dreamed of an occupation that would have something to do with books. The dream came true with an ironic vengeance.

It was announced by the advertising department that the newly appointed Literary Adviser to Houghton Mifflin Company would 'have the author's point of view.' I did, for a time at least. I knew the months of toil, eye work, head work, leg work, seat of the pants to the seat of the chair work, that went into the making of a manuscript of three or four hundred pages, and treated such with respect. I never lost one — at least not permanently. I remembered that Constable of Edinburgh had said, 'By God, I am all but the author of the Waverley Novels,' and that Sir Walter Scott in rebuttal had called publishers 'the pack-horses of Literature.' My view of the case was closer to Sir Walter's than to Constable's. Poe, who had little reason to admire the tribe of Barabbas, had said that a publisher, 'trying to be critical, talks about books pretty much as a washerwoman would about Niagara Falls.' I hoped that enough of the author's point of view lay dormant within me to make me continue to be aware of the majesty of the cataract. Much later, I read in a letter from John Jay Chapman to his wife written after a first heavy conference that, for a publisher, I had something surprisingly 'near to an education and a mind.' But perhaps, as used to be said of the inventor of near-beer, Chapman was a poor judge of distance.

I missed the act of writing and for a year or two suffered from the malaise that follows the non-fulfillment of function; but there were new satisfactions and compensations. Criticism and literary biography are, after all, small business beside imaginative literature — poetry, serious fiction, and the lofty enterprises of history. One came to find a deeper pleasure in the association that a publisher has with all sorts of men and women, poets, novelists, thinkers, writers and makers of history. The publisher meets them on the practical plane of the contract for signature and the copyright statement with check enclosed, yet he is often the confidant of their ambitions, disappointments, and hopes. He shares the inner lives of better men than himself. If they have a common sport, fishing perhaps, there exist twin piers, indoor and outdoor, on which may be erected the edifice of a lifelong friendship.

Few pleasures can surpass the discovery or first recognition of a new and different talent in some unsolicited manuscript or chance meeting; the tending and fiscal watering of it, the public showing, the final full flowering of a hardy perennial. Encourager les autres, c'est faire remonter la pendule de l'existence.

Fortunately for my contentment in this new work, the consulship of Taft, in which it began, saw the dawn of a renaissance of literary expression in America. Its day-rim was soon visible from Park Street.

In free-lance days, I had reviewed a thin volume of verse, of which one piece had haunted my memory. It ended with a strain of New-Celtic mysticism:

> How sure a thing is Beauty,
> I cried. 'No bolt can slay,
> No wave or shock despoil her,
> No ravishers dismay . . .
> The granite hills are slighter,
> The sea more like to fail;
> Behind the rose the planet,
> The Law behind the veil.'

Not all the words are inevitable, but the last two lines had teased my imagination for half a decade, when one day the author turned up on Park Street; a fresh-faced, broad-browed, plain-speaking young woman, standing her ground with a singular solidity — Willa Sibert Cather! Although a poet and the author of brilliant short stories, she was S. S.

McClure's right-hand man on the staff of the magazine that bore his name. She had come to Boston to collect material for one of the magazine's continued feature stories, a biography of Mary Baker G. Eddy. Boston took kindly to her, and she to Boston. A letter from Woodberry reports, finding her visiting Mrs. Fields, that 'she was pleasant to talk to and have about.' So the F. G.'s found her. So, more than all others, perhaps, did Sarah Orne Jewett.

In re-reading the thirteen volumes of the collected edition, one perceives how all of Willa Cather's work is of a piece; how her early training in getting up a subject and planning its exposition gave veracity and *ordonnance* to her fiction; how the sense of beauty which found its first expression in poetry persisted and colored all her work. One wonders whether she, like those other poet-novelists, Hardy and Meredith, might in the age of Elizabeth or the Revolution have been poet only.

In one of her rare, discreet excursions in autobiography, she has spoken slightingly of her first novel, *Alexander's Bridge,* as 'the result of meeting some interesting people in London,' that later it seemed to her 'unnecessary' and 'superficial.'

Perhaps the tragic end of Bartley Alexander, the bridge-builder, drowned in the collapse of his own bridge, is theatrically contrived, but surely Hilda Burgoyne, the Irish actress, first of her unforgettable women — Alexandra Bergson, Thea Kronberg, Antonia Shimerda, Marion Forrester, Lucy Gayheart, Sapphira Colbert — is by no means the least convincing and appealing. Miss Cather's women have more *élan vital* than her male protagonists, yet no novelist has surpassed her in the presentation of those wise observers and kindly commentators who serve the useful purpose of inspiring the leading characters to confession, and forestall the reader in his own reflections. Professor Lucius Wilson in *Alexander's Bridge* is a worthy forerunner of Euclide Auclair, the apothecary-philosopher of *Shadows on the Rock*.

The triangular world of Bartley and Winifred Alexander and Hilda Burgoyne, in Boston, New York, and London, was the world of the novels of Henry James and Edith Wharton, not that real and earthy world which she was soon to make her own by eminent domain. In her introduction to *The Best Stories of Sarah Orne Jewett,* she writes:

'In reading over a package of letters from Sarah Orne Jewett, I find this observation: *"The thing that teases the mind over and over for years, and at last gets itself put down rightly on paper — whether little or great; it belongs to Literature."* Miss Jewett was very conscious of the fact that when a writer makes anything that belongs to Literature (limiting the term here to imaginative literature, which she of course meant), his material goes through a process very different from that by which he makes merely a good story or a good novel. No one can exactly define this process; but certainly persistence, survival, recurrence in the writer's mind, are highly characteristic of it. The shapes and scenes that have "teased" the mind for years, when they do at last get themselves rightly put down, make a very much higher order of writing, and a much more costly, than the most vivid and vigorous transfer of immediate impressions.'

The shapes and scenes that had been teasing her own mind were on the prairies of Nebraska. Thither she returned —

> How smoothly the trains run beyond the Missouri,
> Even in my sleep I know when I have crossed the river —

and wrote *O Pioneers,* as she says, entirely to please herself.

It pleased the critics and the public too, as did its successor *The Song of the Lark,* but it was *My Antonia,* the final expression of 'a persistence, survival, recurrence' that gave me the most thrilling shock of recognition of the real thing of any manuscript that ever came under my eye. I informed the Pow-Wow:

'Antonia has the freshness and vitality of the new soil from which she springs, the vigor of the great prairies in which her vivid and enthralling personal drama unfolds.'

The Pow-Wow took it calmly, but agreed to the favorable contract suggested. Miss Cather now thinks *Antonia* an 'old-fashioned, romantic, and badly constructed tale,' but I suspect that whether artistic black sheep or not — I do not agree that it is — the book is close to the author's heart, as it has been to the hearts of two generations of American readers.

The choice of the 'best' book by a favorite author makes an edifying parlor game. Many good judges would put *A Lost Lady* or *My Mortal Enemy* in the top place, others equally competent who prefer *Death Comes for the Archbishop.* For myself, I read *Shadows on the Rock* oftener and with keener relish than any other, even *Antonia.* I read it once while a guest at the Citadel, which sits on the very tip-top of the Rock. From the windows of my room, called the Murray Room after the first British Governor-General, I looked across the broad St. Laurent to the distant Megantic Mountains, over which Benedict Arnold wormed his stubborn way. To the left, downstream, flanked by the Laurentians, the Isle d'Orléans of my earliest memory divided the current like the prow of a ship. Some hundreds of feet beneath me, the Lower Town, oblivious of the great historic panorama above, bustled about its business as it had in the days of Frontenac.

No other book that I had ever read so completely recaptured the spirit of a place as that I held in my hand. The dingy sail of a small schooner appeared around the island's port bow. Cold chills of excitement ran up and down my spine. It might have been the spring's first ship from France bringing food and farming implements and news of the fighting on the Flanders plain. I finished the re-reading late at night, very late for me, and looked out over the starlit river — experiencing quite literally the echoing Virgilian line:

'Sunt lacrimae rerum et mentem mortalia tangunt.'

Shadows on the Rock is a book of only three hundred-odd pages of large type, the size of a typical adventure or murder or love story that one gulps down between dinner and bedtime, yet it is a full day's reading. Even a paragraph jumper reads it slowly, word by word, each to be savored for its meaning or memory or picture. The corrected first drafts of the Cather novels are marvels of creative revision. For the most part, the style is toned down rather than up. In the rough draft of *Shadows on the Rock,* the sun comes up over the Isle d'Orléans 'like a bridegroom coming out of his chamber.' In the revision it comes up 'over the Isle d'Orléans'; engaging evidence that she, too, composes with fury. Sentences are trimmed, words, phrases, clauses, even paragraphs, omitted. The purgation of superfluities is structural as well as stylistic. She tells with pride that the excised paragraphs and chapters of *Sapphira and the Slave Girl,* put on the bathroom scales, weighed six pounds. In the end, even Dante is hardly a greater master of the magical word too few. The lucid style is the perfect expression of just and lucid thought.

An English critic has said: 'There is nothing to fear, nothing to shrink from, in Miss Cather's work. It is not anger or horror or disgust that she feels when she looks at humanity, but intense, firm sympathy . . . she makes obscure men masters of their destinies, but with all her kindness is never false to reality, never noisier or sadder or sweeter than life.'

It is well put, but perhaps with a little confusion between the quality of the perceiving mind and the phenomena observed. To me her books, though never noisier or sadder or sweeter than life, do sometimes seem saner than the life I have watched from my Park Street window. Perhaps Willa Cather may grasp better than I that law behind the veil.

CHAPTER 13

Amicus musarum

AS THE FIRST DECADE of the twentieth century drew to a close, life seemed to spread out in new directions to all points of the compass. The small tall house on West Cedar Street — four flights of stairs in front, and six in back — was exchanged for one in newly built Charles River Square, demanding less of a climb to go to bed. It abutted on the garden of Mrs. Fields. She took an interest in the proceedings, suggested the name of the property, and, in a friendly clause in her will, left her garden with its lilac hedge planted by Charles Dickens as a playground for the children of the Square.

I began to get around my own country, to spy out the writing circles of Philadelphia, Washington, and Chicago, and to spend a week of each month in New York. There one met the literary veterans of the metropolis — Mark Twain, Richard Watson Gilder, Edward Burlingame, Edmund Clarence Stedman, Henry M. Alden, W. C. Brownell. They had a quick-witted readiness in dealing with any occasion that I hadn't encountered in Boston, but, with the exception of Mr. Clemens, who spent his working day smoking in a bed with a row of cupids in full relief on its footboard, and

Brownell taking his time over his billiard shots at the Century, they always seemed, even in their sixties and seventies, just a little hurried. They lacked the poise and authority I had found in their more leisured coevals on the banks of the Charles. New York was becoming a more important publishing centre than Boston. The leading British authors of the day — Kipling, Stevenson, Conrad, Mrs. Humphry Ward, Wells, Galsworthy — all published there. On the island of Manhattan adventurous young publishers were setting up, who were quicker to welcome the fresh indigenous thing than the older, larger houses in either city; and it was the reviewers of New York, not those of Boston, who now held the scales of literary success or failure.

A week in New York was a mental tonic. Most stimulating of its opportunities were the lunches and dinners at the long table at the Century Club, of which I became a member at a comparatively tender age. There was to be found give-and-take conversation on every conceivable or inconceivable subject, with the man on your right and left, or across the table. He on your left might turn out to be a bishop, he on your right an ambassador; the delightful fellow across the way usually proved to belong in the club's jealously administered category of 'amateur.' The rooms of the Stanford White house have a haunted mellowness, the ghostly body and bouquet of old talk.

The National Institute of Arts and Letters, into which I was admitted about the same time, under the mistaken impression that I was going to be an author, was not always so inspiring. In 1908, it was composed chiefly of the rear guard of that polite school of American letters which had begun in New York with Irving and Willis, nearly a century before.

At one of its public meetings, Hamlin Garland, insurgent

son of the middle border, arose and in a hog-calling bass
voice said:

'Mr. President, I want to propose a motion. I move that
in the home of every member of this great National Institute
of Arts and Letters there shall be a bookcase containing every
work ever written by every member of the great National
Institute of Arts and Letters, and none other.'

Hardly was he again in contact with his seat before Harrison Morris was up.

'Mr. President,' he said in a high Philadelphia tenor: 'I
propose an amendment to Mr. Garland's motion. That over
that bookcase shall be hung a facsimile of the inscription on
Shakespeare's tomb, "Good friend for Jesus' sake forbear to
dig the dust enclosed here." '

Laughter was almost, not quite, unanimous, and the motion, I think, was never put. The Institute is different now.
Its standards have become not lower but higher. It is becoming prompt to recognize the good new thing, however little
it may resemble the good old thing.

In the midst of these itinerant activities came an urgent
call from old Elihu Vedder in Rome for assistance in the
selection and arrangement of 'a barrel of manuscript' that he
had scribbled and illustrated for an autobiography, which
he was calling *The Digressions of V.* It was a job after a seagoing heart. Vedder's pictures for Fitzgerald's *Rubaiyat,* done
on the so-called half-profit basis, and published twenty years
before, had netted each party close to what we should now
describe as a hundred grand, and it was hoped that *The
Digressions* would be equally useful. They were not, but
they gave me a month in the Eternal City and one psychological experience worthy of Titianesque efforts.

During my visit in Rome, Wilbur Wright turned up there with the biplane that he had been demonstrating before the crowned heads of Europe. One afternoon, in a landau drawn by two prancing black horses, sitting with my back to them, facing a beautiful contessa and the Silenic form and features of Vedder, I was driven some miles out on the Campagna. The carriage took its place in a dress-circle of the Roman world. In the foreground lay a few acres of grassy field, through the middle distance marched the ruined aqueduct of Claudian, across the background stretched the purple peaks of the Alban Mountains.

A tall slim figure was working over the plane that looked less like a bird than a small misplaced covered bridge. The figure climbed into it. The motor was started; irregular explosions sent flocks of real birds winging off for Tivoli. It began to crawl along the ground, the pace quickened, it traversed the field. Suddenly, as it seemed with a wrench — certainly there was a wrench in one heart as gravity that makes the apples fall was mastered — *it left the ground!* Three times it circled the field at a height of perhaps thirty feet, and slid down to a bumpy stop. The ancient aqueducts looked more ancient, more ruined than before. After the Icarian dreams of Leonardo and Roger Bacon, air-mindedness, at long last, was born.

I had been at once charmed and alarmed by the internal combustion engine. Now I had learned that, like all God's chillen, it's got wings.

Coming home from Rome via Paris and London, I read Virgil to pass the time in the *wagon-lit* and enrich the memory of the city I had just left. At one point in the journey, a little bored by the continuous mêlée of the later books, I was moved idly to consult the *Sortes Virgilianae*. I stuck my

pocket pencil into the volume and, on opening it, found the
point resting on:

Tum Tartarus ipse
Bis patet in praeceps tantum tenditque sub umbras,

which, as I was presently precipitated into the Mont Cenis
tunnel to spend twenty minutes in Tartarian darkness,
wasn't too bad.

It became a habit for a time to prick the *Aeneid* and see
what was brewing. I even carried the technique into the
examination of a manuscript. If, when pricked, it bled, I
read it at once myself; if only sawdust exuded, I left it to
the first reader.

One day, I saw lying on the table in the outer editorial
room a messy-looking pile of flimsy that obviously had been
the rounds of the learned brothers in New York. Its title, suggestive of eccentric literature, was *Queed*. Nothing, super-
ficially, could have been more forbidding. Nevertheless, willing as always to take a chance, I picked up a paper-cutter
and stabbed the repulsive object. There was a considerable
amount of front matter and the point pierced the thin paper
just between two sentences on the first page of text:

'Down the street came a girl and a dog, rather a small girl
and quite a behemothian dog. If she had been a shade
smaller, or he a shade more behemothian, it would have been
a parody on one's settled idea of a girl and a dog.'

It bled! I read on, it bled some more. Taking it back to
my own room, I read two or three hundred of its six hundred pages, carried it home in my Boston bag and finished
it at midnight. The spring list had been definitely closed
the week before, but, within forty-eight hours, *Queed* was
accepted and on it in the leading position. Its reception by

the reviewers was piebald. The dailies and weeklies thought well of it. The Olympian monthlies held conflicting views.

The *Atlantic* said: 'It is full of vitality, and of clean and wholesome humor. There is in it no shade of weariness, no touch of decadence, but a contagious faith in life, and in the good of human nature.'

The *North American Review* said: 'The book is under-bred from cover to cover. It is compact of provincial out-look, vulgar tone, flippant thinking, and sordid living.'

The reading public sided with the *Atlantic,* and more than a quarter-million copies were sold. Editors who had given short shrift to Henry Sydnor Harrison's short stories eagerly tried to get them back. They tried in vain; a Southern gen-tleman was no worshipper of the 'Bitch-Goddess.' It was rumored that there were scenes in the publishing offices that had returned the obese manuscript of the novel with per-functory expressions of desire to see more of the author's work. There is something in the misfortunes of even our best friends that does not wholly displease us!

Re-read now, after the lapse of a third of a century, *Queed* still has the power to absorb, amuse, and deeply move. The whimsical, roundabout De Morgan manner is dated, as in-deed it had been when De Morgan wrote. Hodder and Stoughton declined *Joseph Vance* — later joyfully accepted by Heineman — on the ground that the public was no longer attracted by the leisurely, roundabout manner of Thackeray. But in Harrison's hands it came back to vigorous life. The development of little Doc Queed from the parody of a prig, to a passionate and effective humanitarian, was a new and timely kind of success story. The sordid living that annoyed the *North American Review* disturbed Queed even more, and the reader knew that after his tale was told Queed, now revealed as Joseph G. Surface, Jr., would do something about it.

As its core, the book was a farewell to the Old South, written by a man who saw the New South in the making. If anywhere in American literature there is a more touching funeral parade of the Confederacy than in the chapter quaintly headed "Queed sits on the Steps with Sharlee, and sees Some Old Soldiers go marching by," I wouldn't know where to find it.

V. V.'s Eyes, and *Angela's Business,* found nearly as many readers as *Queed,* but the law of diminishing return had begun to operate. Both stories were by-products of the impulse that had produced *Queed.* Then came the war, with, for the author, ambulance-driving overseas, a year in the Navy, the death of his brother in France, removal from Virginia to New York, and a gregarious but lonely life there. *St. Theresa,* even with its Homeric fight to a finish between hero and heroine, and the satiric *Andrew Bride of Paris,* showed that Harrison never found his true new direction. Perhaps if he had lived further into the yeasty decade of the thirties something different and more important would have come from him. The fellow himself was better than anything he lived to write. He had sat under Woodberry, and like the others, bore the ineffaceable imprint of a personality.

My dealings with poets in the *Nation* brought a rush of versifiers to Park Street. Most of them, particularly those who wished to read their verses aloud, didn't stay long, but the work of Josephine Preston Peabody, Anna Hempstead Branch, Louise Imogen Guiney, and George Cabot Lodge, the house was proud to publish in a quiet way. In 1911, a poet appeared on the scene who had no truck with quietude

— Amy Lowell, the General Grant of the battle of the poetic wilderness.

There is no lack of good critical opinion on Miss Lowell's writing in prose and free verse. There is plenty, perhaps too much, of amusing reading about her eccentric mode of life and Napoleonic methods of publicity. Somewhere within that face and form so closely resembling Holbein's Henry VIII was hidden a heart that the world and the critics missed. She was avid of affection, adventure, life. There was the true lyric cry in her lines:

> I would anything
> Rather than this cold paper:
> With outside the quiet suns on the sides of the
> burgeoning branches
> And inside only my books!

For a dozen years I dealt with her, disagreed with her; fought, capitulated, made up, and smoked the cigar of peace without victory, to fight again; but with never a break in confident friendship. When she died, it was as if a force of nature had been turned off.

Her published work poetic and polemic, listed in thirteen pages of small type at the back of her biography, is imposing. It performed a timely service for our literature. The work of the 'cosmic poets' never looked quite the same to us again. But in retrospect a certain impermanency in the work of all the Imagists becomes evident.

Its brief life may have been due to its unquotability. Perhaps this came not so much from its lack of mnemonic aids of regular rhythm and recurrent rhyme as from the failure of the Imagists to achieve consistently the sixth and final item of their own creed: 'Concentration is of the very essence of poetry.'

In practice 'concentration' became confused with 'concision.' Their pictorial pieces seem contrived in coolness. They seldom achieved the concentrated heat generating fusion of thought and feeling, memory and imagination, that creates the unforgettable lines like Yeats'

> I hear lake water lapping with low sounds by the shore;
> While I stand on the roadway or on the pavements gray,
> I hear it in the deep heart's core.

One is hard put to it to quote from memory any single line of Imagist poetry. It is the poetry that we can carry about with us in our own minds, to draw on for mental quick ones as stimulant or anodyne, that seems to live longest in the libraries and anthologies.

After the Imagists, my frequentation of the Muses' bower, save for a term on the Pulitzer Prize Committee for Poetry, came to an end. The First World War, the Dividend Decade, the Great Depression, immersed me in prose.

Part Four

Part Four

CHAPTER 14 ~

The old war: First half

THE INVASION OF BELGIUM by the goose-stepping grey
armies of Von Kluck on the night of August 4, 1914, was
less of a surprise to me than to many of my fellow citizens.
The battle legends of Great-aunt Amanda, and early porings
over the pictured scenes of the Rebellion, had made war real
to the imagination. I did not grow up feeling, as most contemporaries seemed to feel, that peace was the permanent
condition of the maladjusted modern world. After the encounter with Wilhelm II on the terrace at Taormina, sinister
portents came to notice. In 1909, the lady on my right at
dinner in London told me of a recent conversation with the
sabre-rattler at an English country house. They were walking together through the long gallery, admiring the pictures,
objects of art, treasure-trove from lands of palm and pine.

Wilhelm's quick eye took it all in appreciatively, and he
said: 'What wonderful things you have in these old English
country houses.'

Then, after a short, reflective pause: 'But of course you
have never been looted. '

She inquired: 'Were you thinking of doing it, sir?'

He replied, 'Who knows, who knows?'

In 1911 came the affair of the German gunboat *Panther* at Agadir in Morocco, looking hopefully for the trouble *agents provocateurs* had been paid to stir up, and a shooting war began between Italy and Turkey in Tripolitania. Early in 1912, in England, I read Erskine Childers' ominous *Riddle of the Sands,* and attended a performance of *An Englishman's Home,* in which the Englishman did what he never had a chance to do in 1914, but pretty much what he did do in 1940. Fresh from these experiences, I spent a weekend at Lady Stanley's hospitable house, Furze Hill in Surrey, where the grounds were laid out as a map of Africa with pools and rivulets named from the lakes and rivers of the dark continent. Sunday afternoon I was awakened from a post-prandial nap by the sound of the firing of small arms under my window. Arising and descending in haste, I found the entire party prone on the lawn blazing away, with sub-calibre rifles, at a row of targets, and was informed: 'This is to repel the German invasion. They are doing it at every country house in England.'

Invited to participate, a squirrel-shooting youth came to my aid. The bull's-eye seemed to attract bullets like a magnet. A young man from the War Office inquired with great interest, "Do all Americans shoot like you?" and was modestly assured that this was nothing compared with the standard proficiency of the countrymen of Deerslayer and Daniel Boone.

Before the year was out, Bulgaria, Serbia, and Greece were at it against Turkey. In three months they appeared to have won, and a book by an Austrian war correspondent, *With the Victorious Bulgarians,* was in press at Riverside. Before it could be put on the market the London Peace Conference had broken down and they were at it again. The day after a treaty was finally signed, they were up for a third round, this time with the Serbs and Greeks fighting the Bulgarians, who were far from victorious. The book celebrating them ran into hard going and accumulated a handsome debit balance. From this, I learned that the best time to publish a war-book is the day you accept it.

Just before the Christmas of 1912, there arrived in the office a tidy manuscript entitled *Pan Germanism*, by Roland G. Usher, a young professor of history at Washington University in St. Louis.

It was a powerful and convincing statement of the imminence of an acute European disturbance.

It was rushed through Riverside and published in February, 1913. The American press expressed a mild academic interest. The *Nation*, under a new, rather pacifist control, condemned it as 'a mass of dogmatism and prognostication.' In England, the general attitude was 'Hush, hush, let the dog lie!' Between February, 1913, and July, 1914, a few hundred were sold. From August to December of the latter year, the distribution approached the classic figure of one hundred thousand copies.

Through the whole month of August, 1914, I was kept out of circulation in villeggiatura at Cohasset by the joint incidence of the unwarlike maladies of whooping cough and mumps. I read the morning and evening papers, Zola's *La Débâcle,* and the five volumes of Napier's *Peninsular War,* and tried to work out what a World War would mean to the publishing business. By early September, Manoury had led into action, in taxicabs, the first internal combustion-engined army in history, Foch, his right and left shattered, his centre in retreat, had attacked, the Germans had been held at the

Marne, and I was back in the office with a pretty clear picture of a publisher's job in wartime.

Before the Old War, there was no such preparation of the world mind for hostilities as that provided, through the thirties, by the war lords of Germany and Japan. The Balkans, puppets or prey of the Dual Monarchy, had played with matches in the powder magazine of Europe, but to all save a few Americans it seemed just another 'European mess,' minor and remote from their business and pleasure. With the exception of *Pan Germanism* and the work of a few far-seeing journalists like Frank Simonds, there was little in print in this country to throw light on the dark causes of the war. But now the mood of the public seemed to be that expressed in the doughboy song of 1917:

> Good-bye, Maw, Good-bye, Paw,
> Good-bye, mule, with your old hee-haw.
> I don't know what the war's about,
> But you bet, by gosh, I'll soon find out.

It appeared that the publisher's job was to assist in the process — and, since there was then no communication through the ether with the antipodes giving us pictures of global battles as they are fought — to publish books telling not only what the war was about, but what it was like. In December, I prepared a report for fellow directors, setting forth the belief that, as the war spread, the interest of the public, so evident in the mounting sales of *Pan Germanism,* would turn more and more to war-books. I urged that enlightened self-interest, as well as public spirit, demanded that securing or projecting these should be the first order of business for the coming year. It was suggested that I be authorized to take passage for England as early as possible in 1915 to look the ground over on the spot.

The report was approved at all points. It resulted in the publication, during the next four years, of more than a hundred war-books, reaching a total circulation of nearly a million and a half copies. Some of them, perhaps, had a flavor of that 'Allied propaganda' which, during the long, uneasy armistice between wars, was considered by isolationists a heinous offense. I did not feel it so then, nor do I now. I read up the German case and felt the force of their need for living room, but I was convinced of the truth of the startling sentence on the first page of Usher's book: 'The Germans aim at nothing less than the domination of Europe and of the world by the Germanic race.'

I tried to give them their day in court, and secured for publication on Park Street books explaining their position, even books producing sympathy for them as individuals, like Fritz Kreisler's vivid *Four Weeks in the Trenches,* or the *Journal of a German Submarine Commander.* The chief aim, nevertheless, was to try to help educate America to a full knowledge of the evil ambitions that were loose in the world, even if in the end it should lead us to join in fighting them.

Early in February, 1915, the German government announced that a complete submarine blockade of Great Britain would begin on February 18, and that passenger ships suspected of carrying contraband of war would be sunk without further notice. On the twenty-fifth, companioned by Henry Harrison, an early volunteer for the American Ambulance in France, I sailed on the *Franconia* for Liverpool. On the forward deck, in their factory red paint, lay four long six-inch rifles, an equal number of turrets for destroyers, and some hundreds of boxes, their contents about equally divided between bacon and high explosives. For two days, without reducing speed, we steamed through fog; on the third day, cutting down a few knots per hour, through fog and ice. It gave one a queer feeling to look over the rail and reflect that down under that lead-colored surface might be a big tin fish full of amiable sporting fellows like himself, ready and eager to blow him to hell!

The voyage was without incident, save that in fine weather off the Old Head of Kinsale, exactly where she was torpedoed ten weeks later, the *Franconia* met and passed within a mile my old friend of the four auction pools, the *Lusitania* — a noble and, in the light of history, a memorable nautical spectacle.

At Liverpool, the passengers were delayed in landing by the searching examination of the Military Intelligence. There began that long series of affirmations as to whether one was a male or female, white or colored, married or single, the place of his birth and his mother's maiden name, his reasons for being there, that were required at every step of European travel in wartime. A hospital-ship slipped in just behind the *Franconia*. To the boxes of T.N.T. and bacon already on the landing stage were added human matériel of war; — hundreds of wounded men. Some were on stretchers, pale and motionless, some proceeding under their own power on crutches, happy with their tickets to Blighty. Detail was introduced into my pictures of war.

In London, not yet fully blacked out, I found a general mood of hopeful excitement. Lord Kitchener's army was nearing the top of its training. The war would be over by autumn. The Kaiser and his sons would don the Death's Head uniform of the White Hussars and lead a last forlorn hope cavalry charge at Sedan or Waterloo! Plans for permanent world peace were in the making.

Wise old heads, however, thought differently. I lunched one day with Lord Bryce, in Buckingham Gate. After the affectionate reception which is so appealing from very old men, and assurances given that the fishing in the Wildcat River at Jackson had been good last summer and that the Bryce Trail up Moat Mountain was being kept bushed out, we got on to the War, and the trail-maker prophesied, 'This war will last three years longer and will be won with an American army in the field.' In March, 1915, this was hitting it on the nose with remarkable Scotch-Irish accuracy. I could find no one else in London who believed the part about the American army. But the author of *The American Commonwealth,* old friend of Norton and Mr. Justice Holmes, Elihu Root and Theodore Roosevelt, knew what he was talking about.

Bryce was sitting at the time as chairman of the commission appointed to investigate German 'atrocities,' and talked freely of its work. He was distressed by the gruesome details of the well-attested evidence, but apparently, in his heart, not disposed to push the case too far as an indictment of a nation. In the current war, with its mass murders and rape of continents, we have heard surprisingly little of atrocities on the body of the individual.

From a new friend, Lieutenant-Colonel John Buchan, slight, sandy-haired, high and wide of brow, home on leave from H.Q. in France, I heard an anecdote which completes the picture of an octogenarian stout fellow.

In the winter of that year, when a show was staged at Soissons, Bryce visited the front and Buchan was detailed to take him around. In the course of the tour, a piece of heavy stuff droned through the air and landed with a stomach-sickening thud perilously near them. Following instructions, all threw themselves face down on the ground. Within a few seconds, Bryce erected his white head, twisted it around from side to side surveying the scene, and said:

'When that cools off, I'd like to measure it.'

Other odd items of the rather jolly war as of 1915 churn up in memory:

Walter Page, sitting at the head of the Embassy lunch table on the day he took over the handling of Turkish affairs, wearing rakishly a fez sent him by some humorist in the Foreign Office, looking, with his swarthy complexion and ample nose, completely the Unspeakable Turk; Sir William Osler, at Oxford, an eminent practical joker, telling Sir Edward Currie, C.O. of the Canadian forces, how he had scattered the butts of Russian cigarettes along the right of way at Oxford Station, to support the rumor that Russian troops had passed through; Harrison and myself hearing the sound of rifle fire and rushing out into Suffolk Street, only to discover that a spy was being shot in a new war-play on the stage of the Haymarket Theatre; a great silver Zeppelin floating high over Cockspur Street, seemingly in complete indifference to the popping gunfire from below. Later she fell, a tangled mass of wreckage and charred Boche bodies, somewhere in Kent.

But for the record, such are of less importance than an afternoon with Lowes Dickinson, Fellow of King's College, Cambridge, and author of *The Letters of a Chinese Official*, that William Jennings Bryan thought was by a real Chinaman and replied to as such.

I had long been an admirer of Dickinson's work and had

published his sweetly reasonable, Ingersoll Lecture, *Is Immortality Desirable?* Interested in further work I had invited him to lunch at Garland's one noon in early March. The day was cold and, unaware of the ascetic habits of the guest, I ordered a sustaining meal, duck with salad. A bottle of Burgundy was warming itself by the fire. One o'clock, the appointed hour, came and passed. One-thirty, two. Still no Dickinson. At two-fifteen, I ate most of the duck and drank all of the Burgundy. At three, as I was sitting by the fire, blandly content, Dickinson arrived, apologetic and excited, his lean scholar's face rosy with satisfaction. He had been, he said, for the last four hours, at the Foreign Office, opening to Sir Edward Grey a plan he had conceived for a League of Nations. Grey was impressed and had told him that if he would go to America and get the organization of such a movement initiated there, England would certainly adhere to it.

Tea, with an egg, was commanded from below. While Dickinson ate, I perused a carbon copy of a document in which the idea was succinctly set forth. The scheme for outlawing future war by stamping out its first spark with united military force differed little from the future Covenant of the League of Nations except that, as I remember it, it depended a little more on the reconciling tongue, a little less on the machine gun. When Dickinson had consumed his ration, we took a piece of paper and jotted down the names of men in America already toying with the idea of a League to Enforce Peace — Lawrence Lowell, C. W. Eliot, Nicholas Murray Butler, ex-President Taft. Dickinson didn't reach the States until January in the following year, and the League to Enforce Peace had been formally organized six months before. His mission brought the thought of English and

American groups together, and prepared the ground for President Wilson's statesmanlike adoption of the idea in the summer of 1916.

Some years later, I discussed the question of the paternity of the League with Lord Grey and Colonel House. Both remembered Lowes Dickinson's part in the proceedings and thought that he was the first to christen the composite brain-child of so many different men The League of Nations. It came out, however, in talking with Grey that, as early as December, 1914, he himself had written to Spring Rice in Washington asking him to sound President Wilson on a plan for a post-war Union of Nations to keep the peace by *force majeure,* which, he then said, *could only be successful if the United States would join.*

In November, 1919, I sat in the Senate gallery and listened sadly to a debate on an unintellectual level that could only be described as pettifoggery. The moral and military force of God's country was withheld from the League. Without that, it became possible for a manic-depressive Austrian painter of picture postcards to become the incarnate spirit of revenge for Versailles, revive the Pan-Germanic dream of world conquest, and plunge mankind into a tragedy beyond the power of imagination fully to conceive.

Soon after the episode of the League, I established relations with Wellington House, headquarters of the British Bureau of Information, where a fishing friend, Hugh Sheringham, angling editor of the *Field,* was to be in charge of matters pertaining to books. This became a prolific source of manuscripts for consideration, dealing with the causes, conduct, and aims of the war.

My last long weekend in England was spent with Will

Meredith at Fleet, hard-by Aldershot. On Sunday we had a good run with the H.Q. Beagles; on Monday a look at 'Kitchener's Mob.' I saw a hundred airplanes aloft at one time, and a brigade of cavalry deploying on the plain. It was a noble equestrian sight! They didn't get much riding in France; the heroic Ninth Lancers had that in the retreat from Mons; but they were the nucleus of the Desert Mounted Corps, which was to turn the tide of battle against the Turk.

In an interval of the manoeuvres, I fell into conversation with a sergeant who was standing at ease and searching his clothes for a gasper. His confidence won by the gift of one of Freibourg and Treyer's special products, he became, for a sergeant, communicative. At the end of the interview, I inquired:

'Well, are you going to lick those Germans?'

'Sure, we're going to lick those Germans,' he replied. And then, the light of introspection coming into his eye, 'You see they ain't a military nation like we.'

In a hopeful frame of mind as to progress of the war, I sailed for home at the end of March on the *Tuscania*. At night she pushed through the dark sea, with deck and signal lights completely blacked out. Inside was a full passenger list, and the riot of song, dance, and *amours de voyage* — that enlivened Atlantic crossings in the first half of the Old War. On board with me was redoubtable John Macrae of Dutton's, the only American publisher I encountered for the duration on or over Periscope Pond.

CHAPTER 15

Adams interlude

AT A DINNER at the Century Club in celebration of the obsequies of the Eighteenth Amendment, I found myself at a table for eight, presided over by Walter Damrosch. The personnel included, in addition to the musician and the publisher of sorts, all the typical talents of the club. The conversation was a little slow in starting, and Damrosch, with his eager social touch, suggested that each man in rotation, clockwise, should favor the company with a narrative of his most exciting professional experience. It started off well with a strong blood-curdling tale from a doctor. Rather scared, I tried to think what my most thrilling publishing adventure had really been. The searching spotlight of memory came to rest on the decade of dealings with Henry Adams that reached a climax in the exact middle of the Old War.

Back in 1907, I had been a guest for a day or two in the hospitable house of the Gilders on Tenth Street. One evening, Gilder came in from the office of the *Century Magazine* with a large flat package. He exposed its contents and said, 'This is a funny book I've just had from the author. It's called *The Education of Henry Adams*. Henry Adams wrote it. I can't make out whether it's all autobiography, or what.'

It was indeed a funny book; out-size, on paper of the most

expensive quality, inordinate margin, a paucity of front matter, no copyright notice.

As was my way with manuscripts, I pricked it in two or three places. It bled — profusely, a bookish hemophilia the like of which I had never seen before. I took it to bed and read it nearly all night. Next morning, instead of the New Haven to Boston, I took the Pennsylvania to Washington. With an audacity that now seems colossal, I rang the bell at the Adams door of the umbilically connected Hay-Adams residence, and asked an aged colored butler if I could see Mr. Adams, was ushered into a drawing room where all the chairs were of nursery altitude, and requested to wait.

Presently the author of the *Education* appeared, small, scraggly-bearded, coolly polite.

'Mr. Adams,' I said, struggling with an untimely return of my adolescent stammer, brought on by excitement, 'I have just finished reading your *Education*. It is one of the great books of the new century. Houghton Mifflin Company want to publish it.'

'I only printed a hundred copies of that book for my friends,' said Mr. Adams. 'I don't know how you got hold of it!'

The ensuing conversation was less prickly than its beginning, but all suggestions of publication were definitely dismissed. Long after, I discovered how very malapropos the proposition was. In that very month, Henry Adams, writing to a friend of the bad state of American letters, had said, 'I am in hopes a kind of esoteric literary art may survive, the finer and happier for the sense of privacy and abandon.'

On the whole, he had dealt kindly with the brash invader of his abandon.

From many a river I had learned that the way to capture

a wise old reluctant trout is to keep after him; to compel him to rise, if not from appetite, perhaps, at last, from irritation.

As tactfully as possible, I kept after Henry Adams. Ralph Cram persuaded the evasive author to permit the publication on Park Street of *Mont Saint-Michel and Chartres,* already privately printed like the *Education,* under the auspices of the American Institute of Architects. The learned, sensuous Mariolatry of the book, the Adams dry light, strained through lovely glass, attracted a wide public. It did very well indeed, as I took extreme satisfaction in reporting to its author. I received an invitation to look in when possible at the twelve o'clock breakfasts, where Henry Adams continued his Education by entertaining beautiful and clever young women, with a sprinkling of men, none too easy in the furniture provided for their occupancy. I made a point of being there once or twice a year, and relished the host's playful sub-acid humor; but though I cast many and various flies, made not the slightest progress toward eliciting a rise.

At last, the negotiation crystallized in correspondence. On December 22, 1915, I wrote:

'The rumor has reached the writer's ears that you are seriously considering the question of finally publishing *The Education of Henry Adams.*

'As I think you know, the honor of issuing this book has long been desired by this house and the matter has been quite recently in our minds because of what seems to be a definite demand for the book in certain quarters occasioned by allusions to it in Thayer's *Life and Letters of John Hay.* May we not, following our publication of *Mont Saint-Michel and Chartres,* now have the privilege of issuing your autobiographic book? It would be a special pleasure to us if, following the publication by us next spring of the *Autobigraphy of Charles Francis Adams* with the Introduction by Senator Lodge, we could announce the publication in the autumn of *The Education of Henry Adams*.'

After some weeks came the reply that has been printed in his collected letters:

'The *Education* was written ten years ago and put into type, tentatively, to be circulated, for correction or suggestion, among the persons interested. Not one — except Charles Eliot — ever returned the volume or offered me a word of advice, and I was still waiting, in 1912, quite unable to cope with my difficulties, when I was suddenly struck down by an illness which put an end to all thought of further literary work.

'Nothing could be done. I could not let the thing go, in its incomplete, uncorrected, tentative form; I could not destroy or suppress it; I could not let anyone else touch it. I could only sit still! and trust to time to forget it.

'Now comes Thayer, and with the overpowering magic of Abraham Lincoln and John Hay calls us all back to life. Unfortunately, I am really dead — stone coffin cold — and cannot go on with the old life. You may as well talk to Lincoln or Hay themselves, or to my father, or any other stone figure. I am not the same animal, and cannot imitate it.

'Meanwhile, there is the volume — scores of copies — floating all over the continent, and Europe too, liable to be taken by anyone, for it is not copyrighted, and already printed in extracts by half the biographies of the time. The book is, as I have said, not in a condition to appear as a work of mine. My idea of what it should be proved beyond my powers. Only St. Augustine ever realized it. Yet I cannot recast or remodel it, and certainly will not publish it as it stands.

'I see only one of two recources, either to pirate it outright, avowedly without my knowledge, or, better, to wait a few months till I am gone, and then do what you like, much as Cram did with the *Chartres*. My own views never go more than three months ahead, but even a year is not long. As for public interest in the subject, you will not imagine it to be real, except in regard to Lincoln. For me, the public does not care a straw — or, I should say, a thousand copies.'

The notion of avoiding the impasse by outright piracy was an old one with him. He tells in the *Education* that he took an article on the gold conspiracy to Edinburgh because 'Adams wanted to escape the terrors of copyright. His highest ambition was to be pirated and advertised free of charge.'

The idea, however, did not appeal in Park Street. I took the train to Washington. There I found the object of the long pursuit in a singularly amiable and obliging, if slightly fantastic mood. The old trout was beginning to stir. He said:

'You have been a great nuisance to me for nearly ten years. I have decided to punish you, and make the punishment fit the crime. I am arranging to leave the *Education* to the Massachusetts Historical Society. When I am dead, you can publish it for them. You will lose your money on it. That will be your punishment. You won't have long to wait. My doctor told me yesterday that I can't live over a month.'

This was not an easy speech to reply to. I did the best I could and came away. A desire to button things up led me to write from Boston:

'I am writing to confirm our conversation of last Friday in regard to the publication of *The Education of Henry*

Adams. My understanding is that when the proper moment arrives, which we trust may be long delayed, we are authorized to manufacture and publish this book in conjunction with the Massachusetts Historical Society, and with a Preface and Introduction by W. R. Thayer.

'If you will be good enough briefly to acknowledge and confirm this understanding, so that the record may be complete, we shall be very greatly obliged.

'I have ventured to report this arrangement to Thayer, and also to Worthington Ford, who chanced to call at my office yesterday on another matter, both of whom are very greatly pleased thereby.'

By return I received the following in the large round Adams hand:

'Thanks for your obliging letter of the 15th. I am unfortunate in my way of expressing myself. Perhaps I have reached an age when I had better not try.

'What I meant to say was that, during my life I should not publish the *Education*. I preferred to leave it as it stood. That after my death I should leave my attested copy to the Massachusetts Historical Society to do what they pleased with. You could make what arrangement you liked with them. I added that I should interpose no obstacle.

'Since receiving your letter, I must qualify this statement. I shall express wishes which may be obstacles. Please bear in mind that for reasons personal to myself, I do not want publication. I prefer the situation as it stands. Under no circumstances will I bind myself to publish or to help publication. If you drop the matter altogether, I shall be satisfied.

'Still, I admit that there is a point where a man makes a fool of himself by chasing crotchets, and commonly he reaches that point when he is buried.'

I saw that, in asking for confirmation, I had introduced a jarring note of explicitness. The fish had felt the hook and was off. Or was he? On February 19, I wrote:

'Thank you for your letter of February 18th. I am sorry if I in any way misunderstood your position in regard to the publication of *The Education of Henry Adams*. Personally, I should be extremely loath to take any steps at any time toward the publication of a book against the wishes of its author — except, perhaps, in a case like this, where, as it seems to me, the literary loss to the world through non-publication would be so serious as perhaps to counterbalance one's personal feelings.

'I understand now that the book is to be left to the Massachusetts Historical Society, to do with it as seems best to them. I think that we can depend upon the council of that body to act only in a discreet and statesmanlike manner.

'I am sorry if my urgency has been in any way an annoyance to you, but I hope you will believe it has sprung, not from commercial motives, but from a profound personal admiration and liking for the book, and the conviction that it is so significant a document in our intellectual history that to withhold it forever from publication would be a disaster.'

Happily, the medical prognosis was wrong. Henry Adams lived two full years more, the Washington breakfasts continued, and he took each summer the spacious country house that stands at the head of Tyringham Valley in the Berkshires, filling it with the young life that he liked to have around him.

In the autumn of 1918, *The Education of Henry Adams* was published by Houghton Mifflin Company, who have not lost any money on it yet. Nor have I ever felt any twinges of a tender conscience for printing it against the so strongly expressed wishes of the author. Virgil, we are told, on his deathbed asked his friends to bring in the only manuscript of the *Aeneid* that he might with his own eyes watch it burn. They refused, but promised by all their gods that it would never be published. I at least had never held out that false hope.

I have read the book through at least once every five years since publication, finding in it more to think about with each reading.

It ends with the mild expression of a faint hope that perhaps the three friends, King, Hay, and Adams, might return on the centennial of their birth, 1938, and 'find a world that sensitive and timid natures could regard without a shudder.'

One hates to think what Adams would have thought of the world in the year of Munich, and doubts whether John Hay, discouraged about 'progress' to begin with, and 'tired,' as he once told a young inquirer about Lowell, 'to the very marrow of my bones,' would have shuddered less. Perhaps only Clarence King, most vital and eupeptic of the three, would not have been convinced that evolution had permanently gone into reverse, that the Steam Engine and the Dynamo had finally and forever prevailed over the Virgin.

For the intellectual history of the United States, there is no better basic text than the ample personal records of the Adams family, covering more than a century and a half, from the Revolution through the First World War. If John Adams, completed by his Abigail, was the archetypical, Henry was surely the quintessential Adams, refined, and, despite his protests, 'educated' to a point where he became, in Hay's frequent address of endearment, Porcupinus Angelicus.

Yet in spite of the theoretical pessimism of his work, its final effect is the reverse of pessimistic. His twenty long volumes and the thousands of pages of witty, probing, letters, published and unpublished, reveal an intellect whose vigor and industry, by example if not again by precept, enforce the fine speech in his *Democracy:*

'If our age is to be beaten, let us die in the ranks. If it is to be victorious, let us be the first to lead the column. Anyway, let us not be skulkers and grumblers.'

CHAPTER 16

The old war: Second half

MEANWHILE, THE WAR was going on, and things were stirring on the home front. George Macaulay Trevelyan, author of *Garibaldi and the Thousand,* who had been in Serbia, spark-plug of the explosion, was writing a book about the heroic resistance of the Serbs, and came to America to tell us what the war was like. On the seventh of May, 1915, we climbed Chocorua Mountain together. It proved quite a business for me. Muttering *non sum qualis eram,* I struggled to keep within sight of my companion, a mighty member of the Alpine Club, who forsook the trail to scale all the adjacent cliffs. On the needle-like peak, the Indian fire warden met us with startling news heard over the wire that stretched from tree to tree up the mountain's western slope. The *Lusitania* had been torpedoed and sunk off the Irish coast. More than a thousand passengers, including a hundred American citizens, had been lost.

Disregarding the noble view, Paugus, the toad, and Passaconaway to the west; the stately Presidential Range to the north; misty blue lakes to the east and south; we held a council of war. Trevelyan's engagements called for another month in the United States, but he said, 'I can't stand it, I'm going home now.' We drove back to Boston that afternoon,

and he caught the first boat from New York. On his arrival
in England, he found that the House of Savoy had at last
severed the Triple Alliance, and was in the war on the side
of the Allies. He became, for duration, commandant of the
first British ambulance unit for Italy. There, in the high
mountain fighting, he scaled his cliffs with wounded men
attached.

The war dragged on, the world scene darkened, through
1915, through 1916. Gallipoli, Verdun, the Somme, Jutland;
it began to look like stalemate or worse. Wilson through
Colonel House, his ears and eyes and voice in Europe, moved
for a negotiated peace. Germany was not unwilling; it
would have been a German victory. The Allies, wisely, were
not taking any. At the end of 1916, new cabinets were
organized in England, France, and Italy. Woodrow Wilson,
who had 'kept us out of war,' was re-elected President of the
United States. The future looked black, but I found, as so
many did at that time, that it was agreeing with me. In 1914,
on the verge of forty, doing easily work that was agreeable,
I was contented, too contented, slowly becoming fat and
scant of breath. By the end of 1916, though worried, I was in
better wind.

Good books were coming into Park Street that had nothing
to do with the war, *O Pioneers, The Song of the Lark,*
Thayer's *Life and Letters of John Hay,* Beveridge's monumental *John Marshall;* but it was the war-books that absorbed most of my time and thought; Mildred Aldrich's
*Hilltop on the Marne, The Odyssey of a Torpedoed Trans-
port,* Beith's *First Hundred Thousand,* Lauriat's *The Lusitania's Last Voyage,* Leslie Buswell's *Ambulance Number
Ten;* President Eliot's *The Road to Peace, Kitchener's Mob*

by James Norman Hall. A letter from him when he had transferred into the Lafayette Escadrille, and had his first solo flight, concluded, 'I know now why birds sing.'

In December, 1916, a year after Henry Ford had failed to get the boys out of the trenches by Christmas, I decided that it was time to go to England again.

As before, the German High Command took countermeasures. The day I sailed, January 31, 1917, they announced that 'frightfulness,' the old word for the strategy of terror, was to become completely unrestricted on the seas the following morning. Diplomatic relations with Germany were broken while I was on the water. The *Finland,* a comfortable, mahogany-panelled little ship, had huge American flags painted on either bow, and was brilliantly illuminated at night. Not wholly pleased at having been kept out of war after the *Lusitania,* though I now understand it could not have been otherwise, I suggested to the Captain that a portrait of Mr. Wilson of similar size might be a more effective safeguard. The Captain approved the idea, but amended it. 'Mr. Wilson to starboard, Mrs. Wilson to port.'

The voyage was calm, the evenings quiet. The small ship's company read war-books and history, gravely discussed the war. Off the Irish coast, there was an incident. One afternoon at teatime, a large barque, some three or four miles off the beam to the southward, later reported of Russian registry, was seen to be in trouble. As the stewards and a few passengers who chanced to be on deck watched her, her sails seemed to pitch forward and she slowly sank from sight. The *Finland* changed her course and went away from there as rapidly as possible. Across St. George's Channel stretched a protective line of mine-sweeping trawlers, one every half-mile, as far as the eye could see. At Liverpool, the Intelligence Officer was even more inquisitive than before. In the small hours of the morning, we arrived at a London completely blacked out, a very different London from that I had left two years before.

England had not been blitzed from the air. There were no piles of historic rubble, or long lists of civilian dead. Yet the Old War in its third year was getting hard to take. It lacked the excitement and change of a planetary war of movement — reverses, successes, forays and escapes, invasions and victories, that can be followed fully only on a globe. In 1917, the war was being fought out under the sea and in a single long gash across the face of France. The big guns could be heard in England, as the line swayed back and forth, now ten miles forward, now eight miles back. Casualties were colossal. In the battle of the Somme, Britain had lost four hundred thousand men, sixty thousand in a single day. It was England's second darkest, and perhaps her next to most glorious, hour.

The German submarines were getting in their dirty work with ever-increasing effectiveness. Food was scarce, heat hard to come by. Belts were pulled tighter, deep breathing took the place of glowing fires. It seemed as if the war might last forever. English faces became a little bleak, but never despondent. Dogged does it!

The small group of Americans in London drew together and talked war. *Ense petit placidam sub libertate quietem,* as I said, quoting the motto of Massachusetts, in concluding some post-prandial remarks to the British Publishers' Association. Walter Page at the Embassy, an anxious Page, had to preserve diplomatic discretion, but there was no doubt how he felt about American intervention. Henry van Dyke, another fishing friend, was at Garland's *en route* home after resigning from his Embassy at the Hague. We dined together when other engagements permitted. One night, after we had unearthed the last bottle of Bernkastler Doktor to be found at any wine merchant's, we drank confusion to the Kaiser, success to an American army in the field, and a week of fishing together on the Graach River in the free Duchy of Luxembourg, where van Dyke had done well in the spring of 1914.

For the English the great question, now that diplomatic relations had been severed, was would the Yanks be coming, and how soon? I was asked it brightly by Lady Asquith during the progress of a meagre tea in a cold house on Hanover Square she had taken when dispossessed from 10 Downing Street by Lloyd George; anxiously by Osler at Oxford, whose son Revere, descendant of Paul, had survived the Somme, but was to rendezvous with death on the Ypres salient in August; weightily by Lord French, handsome, white-haired, brick-colored of countenance, in tweeds of the same hue. An affirmative answer and a favorable prognosis as to time may have helped me to secure for publication that general's soldierly narrative, simply entitled *1914*. I was asked the same question by all the sorts and conditions of Englishmen enumerated in an earlier chapter. I had long talks on the subject with Lord Bryce and Gilbert Murray. One day the latter came to Garland's with tremendous news. The Russian Revolution! Bliss it was in that dawn to be alive! Later, it didn't look so blissful, but now it seems we were right the first time.

The brightest memory of that dark, cold, ill-fed winter is of the growth of my friendship with John Buchan, back permanently from the front, and established as Director of Intelligence and Information under the Prime Minister. We

had, we found, things in common; how many, it took a
quarter of a century to discover. We were of precisely the
same age. Buchan, at nine, was easing *Salmo Fario* from the
burns that descend the Tweedside hills at the moment I was
derricking *Salvelinus fontinalis* from the Halfway Brook.
We were both nourished on legends of old wars, Buchan's the
older. We had listened, at Oxford and Columbia, to the
same siren's song. Buchan's Woodberry had been Gilbert
Murray. We spoke the same language — largely Latin, after
dinner. My rather Shandean sense of humor was matched by
Buchan's mildly Rabelaisian turn.

Between Buchan at the Foreign Office and Sheringham at
Wellington House, I came to be informed concerning some
matters that didn't get into the papers. The connection
helped me out of my only difficulty with Scotland Yard. In
1917, Ireland, that most distressful country, saw an opportunity to realize the separatist aspirations of three centuries.
An important Irish lady in London, seeing a possible channel
of publicity for the United States, took to sending me Sinn
Fein bulletins of information in plain sealed envelopes
through the post.

One day, as I was eating my slender breakfast, a waiter
appeared:

'A person below wishes to see you, sir.'

'Oh, very well, show him up.'

He came, a neat-bearded, thick-set person, in bowler hat,
double-breasted blue suit, very heavily soled shoes. It was
more a shock than a surprise when he announced: 'I am
from Scotland Yard.'

I ventured that Scotland Yard was the background of some
favorite reading, and inquired how I could oblige.

'We have been interested in the letters you have been receiving containing Irish information. Would you be so good as to explain them to me, or would you prefer to come over and talk with the Superintendent?'

This was the first intimation that the domestic mail of even friendly aliens in London was being looked into. The prospect of a talk with the Superintendent lacked charm. Without mentioning names, I told the Inspector as much as I thought it was good for him to know, and exhibited memoranda from Buchan and Sheringham that had arrived in the morning's post and were lying on the table in envelopes marked, 'On His Majesty's Business.' This seemed to satisfy authority that I was not an enemy of the British Empire. After inquiring whether the Yanks were really coming, the Law, with a certain majesty of heavy footsteps, departed.

Early in March, Buchan, thin from overwork and an inner malady that gnawed at his vitals, suggested that we spend a long weekend at Dulverton in West Somerset, where, according to the *Fishing Gazette,* February Fill-Dyke had done her perfect work, and fat little moorland trout were rising in the Barle and the Exe. Rather thin myself from fog and fasting and the incubus of war, I fell in with the idea one hundred per cent. Two days before we were to start, word came from Buchan that he was to have an operation instead. His place in the expedition was taken by Romilly Fedden, sound painter and delightful angling writer, home on sick-leave, after having been badly gassed at the end of the battle of the Somme.

For a week we spent our days dealing with willing little trout of the five-to-a-pound variety, along banks of daffodils, amid flocks of newborn lambs that as we approached fled to their bleating mothers for safety and sustenance. After brief evenings around a vast English billiard table, replete with mutton, strawberry tart, clotted cream, and Devonshire cider, we slept the sleep the honest angler knows.

We felt a deep, poignant, half-shamefaced satisfaction on our little island of happiness in the ocean of war. Had one's ancestor, Jeffrey Cooper, felt it on the Halfway Brook in the old French War from the thought of comrades facing musket and tomahawk just a little beyond? Is there not an intensity in Izaak Walton's love for the tranquillity of smooth flowing waters that was engendered from the civil wars?

Back in London, fresher and more fat, I went around to Portland Place to report my information and intelligence of trout to a convalescent Director. I found him in bed, looking noble in his pajamas, no easy feat for modern man, doing, characteristically, four things at once. He was reading proof of both a volume of his own *History of the War* and of Susan Buchan's translation of Paul Géraldy's *La Guerre, Madame;* he was re-reading, for his greater pleasure, Mary Johnston's Civil War novel *The Long Roll;* and he was working on the manuscript of *Greenmantle.* Writing was as natural to him and as constant as breathing.

Toward the end of March, having collected a respectable number of promising manuscripts and exhausted my meat and sugar ration cards, I took passage for home on the *Baltic.* It had been arranged that Bryce and Murray were to sail with me to make speaking tours in the United States. Every other day came a notice from the White Star Line that sailing had been postponed. It was communicated privately that submarines were known to be waiting for her off the Mersey Bar. At last the word was passed that she would sail the following day. That afternoon Gilbert Murray came again to communicate tremendous news. Mr. Balfour had received a code cablegram from Colonel House. The President would ask Congress for a declaration of war on April 6. It was no longer important for Bryce and himself to make the harried crossing.

After pasting labels on the luggage, I went to the Embassy to say good-bye to Page. My impression is clear that the American Ambassador knew less of the full extent of the President's impending message than had been revealed to Balfour by Colonel House. Yet, war-worn and weary from the strain of the last three years, he was radiant with the hope that America must now at last take the field.

Late on the last night in London, a man from the War Office came around. Would I be willing to act as a sort of King's Messenger and carry dispatches to their people in New York? The spirit of Richard Ferris, Messenger of the Virgin Queen, dictated joyful assent. I was given a fat package with imposing seals, that I was prepared to protect with my life.

Next morning at Euston, although I arrived early, the chance of a seat looked slim. The train was full and over-flowing, as only a European train with its side doors can over-flow. After many failures to effect an entrance, the porter laid his hand on the door of a first-class compartment labelled *Reserved*, occupied only by a single large British officer exuding an incredible hauteur, and said, 'Let's try this, sir.' I had my doubts, but when the officer looked up, prepared to repel boarders at any cost of courtesy, he ejaculated, 'By God, it's F. G.!' It was my old friend, Ford Madox Hueffer Ford, in uniform replacing black velvet jacket, a fine figure of a fighting man. The door was firmly locked and we made the trip to Liverpool in great comfort.

In the intervals of an animated conversation, Ford applied himself to two pieces of literary work he had in hand. He read the proofs of an erotic novel he had written in French for publication in Paris, to eke out his captain's pay, and he prepared an elaborate report for his regimental adjutant concerning four blankets missing from his company's quota. At Liverpool, we parted with the customary casual *'Bonne chance!'* Three weeks later, Ford, with his company of Canadians, was among the first over Vimy Ridge.

For three days the *Baltic* lay within the dock, waiting for no one knew what. Each day Intelligence Officers came aboard and departed, taking with them some one of the passengers. The second day, a steward approached and said, 'The Captain's compliments and he would like to see you.' It sounded like trouble. But the Captain turned out to be another old friend of other voyages, 'Tubby' Finch. He proffered a Corona Corona and said, 'I hear you are carrying dispatches for us. Are you comfortable in your cabin?' I said I was, perfectly, but, despite protestation, was transferred to a suite of three rooms and bath.

On the third day, a Sunday, it was announced that we would sail at midnight. The twenty passengers were advised to sleep in their underwear and have life preservers handy, which were to be worn on deck at all times. At sunset, fourteen large ships slipped out and anchored in the stream. At midnight, in pajamas, but with inflatable Gieve waistcoat complete with brandy flask very handy, I felt that we were off.

This was just before the days of the convoy system; indeed, it was that peak week of submarine warfare, in which fifty-seven ships were sunk off the British coast, that brought the new system in. Coming on deck early the next morning, I was surprised to find not another ship in sight. The *Baltic* was proceeding north, within a mile or two of the mountainous coast of Cumberland. At the Mull of Kintyre, she headed west, and lay for two days off the Giant's Causeway behind the Isle of Rathlin. Then, just at dusk, a destroyer came twisting and tossing through a rising westerly gale. There was a megaphone conversation, and the *Baltic* got under way again. Zigzagging every two miles, she made a big Z as well, north to the latitude of Iceland, south to that of Bermuda. 'Tubby' Finch had been sunk the year before in the *Arabic*. Too heavy to be pulled on the life raft, he had been two hours in the cold Atlantic and hadn't liked it. He was taking no chances this time.

Halfway over, news came of America's declaration of war. After sixteen days of zigzagging, without an incident other than daily target practice, and the sudden surfacing of a small whale that found the gun crew on the alert, the *Baltic* passed the Nantucket lightship, and a grey destroyer came along to look us over, the American flag streaming at her stern.

Other flags flaunt themselves bravely in the breeze, but none, sentiment and association aside, is so well designed as ours to impress and inspire. It is not so much the stars as the stripes that do it. Windblown, they ripple and dance, and seem to come ineluctably alive, less a symbol than an incarnation of the spirit of America.

With America fighting overseas, war-books from every angle became still more numerous and important. Through the last nine months of 1917 and the first ten of 1918, I gave little thought to anything else. Soon after I landed from the *Baltic,* the Navy suggested that they could use me in Communications, perhaps in London. It was a terrific temptation, but, after a conference in Washington, the consensus of wise men was that I would better keep on doing my bit where I was. In the summer of 1918, Brigadier-General Marlborough Churchill of G—2 inquired if I would like to be commissioned to go to France with a motor car and an orderly, and tour from one Divisional H.Q. to another, to find the men to write books to bolster civilian and military morale. That, I felt was a job, as Montaigne says, direct to my racket. The papers were in train when the Munich Revolution broke out and the war came to its, as it almost seemed, untimely end.

Just before that, however, I did have some motoring that I shall never forget — driving community nurses to cases in the poorer sections of Boston during the great flu epidemic in October. The sights encountered were as macabre as those described in DeFoe's *The Plague Year*.

In the ground floor of a tenement near Roxbury Crossing we found the body of a young woman, fully clothed even to hat and rubbers, lying on a sofa. No one knew who she was. She had walked in off the street and stretched herself out on the sofa to die. In the Italian quarter in Charlestown, we uncovered two men and two women very ill in one bed. Going back one morning to collect and return an oxygen tank that I had borrowed from a neighboring hospital in the vain attempt to save a handsome bearded man, definitely *in extremis,* I found him neatly shaved and laid out with candles, but not another soul in the house. The neighbors only knew 'they had all gone away.' The epidemic face of war is not its least horrible!

On the day of the false armistice, I had my most bizarre adventure. After being pelted with telephone books thrown from the skyscrapers of New York, I took the train for Washington to see General Churchill. As I was forcing a way through an orgiastic crowd in the concourse of the Union Station, I was embraced and resoundingly smacked by a stalwart colored girl.

The day of the true armistice was different. I lunched with William Roscoe Thayer on Berkeley Street in Cambridge. The other guests were Lawrence Lowell, Lord Charnwood, a French savant who said little and drank much, whose name I cannot recall, and Henry Cabot Lodge, Chairman of the Foreign Relations Committee of the Senate. Through the meal, the conversation dwelt on the probable terms of the armistice. The Senator was concerned lest the softening influence of Wilson might make them too easy. At two o'clock, a spectacled maid came into the room. Washington wanted Senator Lodge on the telephone. 'That,' he said, 'will be my secretary with the terms.'

As he received them, he called them out one by one through the open door from hall to dining room. Immediate evacuation of all conquered territory; an Allied watch on the Rhine; the surrender of five thousand locomotives, five thousand motor lorries, one hundred and fifty thousand freight cars, one hundred and sixty submarines, the whole of their fighting fleet. I inquired, freshly, I am afraid, 'Did they leave them their shirts?' 'Well, no,' said Lodge, at once pleased with the terms and regretful at the failure of his forecast, 'apparently not.'

There was general excitement and rejoicing. I was rather shocked when they had to look it up in the atlas before they could believe that Coblentz was on the left bank of the Rhine.

CHAPTER 17

'Peace'

'WHAT A BEAUTIFUL FIX we are in now!' said Napoleon after the Treaty of Amiens. 'Peace has been declared!' I didn't go as far as that. The return of the mother of the arts was very welcome, but I wondered if we were ready for her. To try to find out, I sailed for Plymouth on the *Rotterdam* early in 1919.

London at night was again a foggy golden glow. The lights that Edward Grey saw going out all over Europe were being re-lit. Night clubs were at their jazzy zenith. I was taken to one, but, suffering from bad air, claustrophobia, and din, recalled with appreciation Clemenceau's reported observation in a similar position:

'On ne voit que des figures qui s'ennuient et des derrières qui s'amusent.'

Yet despite a lifelong disinclination for evening entertainment, I made the tedious journey by tube to Hammersmith to see a play about Abraham Lincoln, drawn from Lord Charnwood's book by John Drinkwater. The house was crowded to the doors — admirals, generals, sailors, tommies, members of Parliament, poets, profiteers, with their ladies and girls, wept through the last two scenes, and when it was over sat quietly in their seats, too spellbound to get up and go home.

As Arnold Bennett wrote: 'Americans will more clearly realize what John Drinkwater has achieved with the London public if they imagine somebody putting on a play about the Crimean War at some unknown derelict theatre round about Two Hundred and Fiftieth Street, and drawing all New York to Two Hundred and Fiftieth Street.'

The great moment of the evening was during the scene at Appomattox Court House:

'*Lee*: You allow our officers to keep their horses. That is gracious. Our cavalry troopers' horses are also their own.

'*Grant*: I understand. They will be needed on the farms. It shall be done.

'*Lee*: I thank you. It will do much towards concilating our people.'

The heterogeneous British audience responded as if with a single sob — evidence of the feeling that was betrayed at Versailles.

Riding back in the tube, rather groggy, it appeared that here was a publishing proposition. Drinkwater was had into Garland's for lunch. Pale, gentle, immaculately groomed, yet somehow ambrosial, the milder Andrew Marvell of our day, he immediately expressed an interest in a roll of fishing rods in the corner. We were attuned. Favorable terms were arranged for both *Abraham Lincoln* and a subsequent volume of collected poems. When I returned to Boston, some three weeks later, with a dignified expense account and nothing to show for immediate publication but a prose play of a hundred pages, eyebrows were raised among fellow directors. As the sale rolled up, eventually exceeding three hundred thousand copies, they were dropped to their normal low level.

The homecoming by transport with troops from Brest found an arid land. The Eighteenth Amendment had been confirmed by the States, and the Volstead Act, defining intoxicating liquor *ad absurdum,* was looming darkly on the congressional horizon. From the beginning an inextinguishable optimist, I believed and maintained that no law contrary to reason and common sense could last forever, but found few to share that hope. Asked by Sheringham, who was editing *The Book of the Fly Rod* for British publication, to contribute a chapter on 'The Fly Rod in North America,' I ventured to include an accounting, from the fisherman's point of view, of that experiment, noble in purpose, that is coming, with the years, to have a nostalgic charm:

'Perhaps the most distressing present difference between fishing in America and in the British Isles lies in the important business of quenching thirst. Anglers have always been connoisseurs in that matter and one of our presidents has said that the mark of the true fisherman is that he draweth not his flask in secret. But consider the sorry case of the American today. His British brother takes a bottle of claret to the streamside, if, as the old fishing book says, "he has a boy to carry it." Failing the boy and the claret, he has only to fish along up to the bridge, where there is sure to be an inn and a mug of bitter to restore him. When the evening rise is over, and the last two-pounder has broken him darkly in the weeds, he returns to a late dinner mitigated by Bristol cream, Rhine wine, more claret, and Burgundy, with a glass of port or old brandy after. Then, when the events of the day have been fully discussed and proper lessons derived from them, he retires to his virtuous slumbers, warmed, if the evening be chilly, by a noggin of hot Scotch or rum.

'Here in this day of wrath our chief recourse for courage

or consolation, even when we have gone over our waders, or lost Leviathan, is gin — gin of our own making, aged during the time consumed in its transfer from the demijohn to the shaker. But we must not complain too loudly. Home-made gin mingled with barbless Vermouth is really not so bad; and there are documents to prove that the juice of the juniper is the traditional drink of the American angler. Listen to Thaddeus Norris in *The American Angler's Book*. He describes in 1864 his preparations for a trip to Colebrook, then as now a well-known fishing station on the Connecticut River:

' "There were three of us: our baggage as follows: Item, one bottle of gin, two shirts; Item, one bottle schnapps, two pair stockings: Item, one bottle Schiedam, one pair fishing-pants: Item, one bottle genuine aromatic, by Udolpho Wolfe, name on the wrapper, without which the article is fictitious, one pair extra boots; Item, one bottle extract of juniper-berry; one bottle brandy, long and wide, prescribed by scientific skill for medicinal purposes. Also, rods, tackle in abundance, and a supply of gin; in addition, each of us had a quart-flask in our pockets, containing gin. We also had some gin inside when we started."

'No wonder he didn't like to fish upstream!'

In September, 1919, came a letter from John Buchan. Lord Grey was coming to Washington on a special mission to deal with questions arising out of the peace pending the appointment of a permanent Ambassador. His sight, impaired by wartime days and nights at the Foreign Office, was failing; he was cut off from many pleasures; fishing talk was his favorite relaxation; if I should be going to Washington, would I call on him. He enclosed a note of introduction.

Armed with this I presented myself at the British Embassy at the earliest possible moment and was received with the warmth of confraternity.

In person, Edward Grey was a handsome embodiment of his race. Slender, well over six feet, when examined some years before at Galton's 'anthropometric laboratory' he was found to have the largest lung capacity on record at that time. A friend wrote him, 'I hear you are the greatest wind-bag out.' His aquiline countenance had no hint of the fierce-ness of the eagle, but only the look of soaring flight, and, pathetically, of far vision.

The effect of his presence cannot be better expressed than in the words of Trevelyan, his biographer:

'Merely to be with him was a heartening experience, be-cause there emanated from him a sense of power in repose, a strength of personality unequalled in any other man whom I have met: but it was quiet strength in enforced subjection to reason, formidable only to folly and attuned to the kindly purposes of common life and welfare.'

As we were talking in Washington, just passing from the chances of the League to the new American method of taking salmon on the dry fly, a secretary came in with the post. On top was an envelope bearing the corner card of Harvard University. 'Hello,' said Grey, 'this looks interesting; do you mind if I open it?' What that led to is documented in a memorandum prepared for Trevelyan and printed in his book:

'He was asked by Lawrence Lowell to come up to Harvard to speak informally to the student body of the University. I happened to be with him in Washington at the time, and he asked me whether *Recreation, its place in a well-ordered life,* with special emphasis on birds and fishes would be suit-

able, and I naturally said it would. Well, without any other
preparation than turning it over in his mind and perhaps
making a few notes, he got up at the Union before a thousand
boys whom I suppose he couldn't see, and talked it off without a pause. We had a stenographer present who took him
down *verbatim*. The copy so produced was sent to him for
revision, but came back with hardly any changes.'

Published under the title *Recreation,* this extempore, un-
revised composition was a marvellous exhibition of the
orderly stores of Lord Grey's mind, and of the training in
public speech that could pour them out with that bright
speed. Take a typical paragraph:

'And now my last discourse shall be on one sentence from
Colonel Roosevelt which I saw quoted the other day. It is
this: "He is not fit to live who is not fit to die, and he is not
fit to die who shrinks from the joy of life or from the duty
of life." Observe that the joy of life and the duty of life are
put side by side. Many people preach the doctrine of the
duty of life. It is comparatively seldom that you find one
who puts the joy of life as something to be cultivated, to be
encouraged on an equal footing with the duty of life. And
of all the joys of life which may fairly come under the head
of recreation there is nothing more great, more refreshing,
more beneficial in the widest sense of the word, than a real
love of the beauty of the world. Some people cannot feel it.
To such people I can only say, as Turner once said to a lady
who complained that she could not see sunsets as he painted
them, "Don't you wish you could, madam?" But to those who
have some feeling that the natural world has beauty in it I
would say, cultivate this feeling and encourage it in every
way you can. Consider the seasons, the joy of the spring,
the splendor of the summer, the sunset colors of the autumn,

the delicate and graceful bareness of winter trees, the beauty of snow, the beauty of light upon water, what the old Greek called the unnumbered smiling of the sea.'

The friendship so begun continued in a constant flow of fishing-cum-publishing correspondence. 'What you say,' wrote Grey, 'makes me sure that you and I have pleasure and feeling in common.' Nearly every letter that came from him contained a report of the fight for vision. In February, 1921, he wrote:

'My bad sight shuts me off from so much that I have not seen Colonel House's article. There is a line about "sad seclusion from decay of sense" which is very applicable to impaired sight. Within the last few days there have been signs that encourage me to hope, but they are as yet very slight and not enough to make any difference to my life. Still, if improvement really has begun it may continue, though it seems too good to be true to think that I shall again be able to fish with a dry fly. That is a long way off yet.'

In April of that year I was in England again and hoped to combine business and pleasure in a few days with Lord Grey on the Cassley, a salmon river in Rosshire. A misadventure with a coal hole on lower Regent Street that left me with a dislocated shoulder and a broken arm prevented that. I didn't miss much in the way of fishing. Grey reported eleven blank days out of thirteen. But to have missed that streamside companionship is one of my bitterest regrets. There was compensation, however, in the long fishing talks over our pipes, often running from lunch to teatime, that I enjoyed throughout the twenties whenever I was in England. Sometimes the talk turned on recent history. Could Bulgaria have been kept out of the war, could the war itself have been avoided had it been possible for the pipe-smoker the other side of the fire to have told Germany that if Belgium were invaded England would fight? It had, of course, not been possible in a Parliament-governed democracy until after the event. Looking back on those conversations, I feel that Grey, in an age when decency was at a discount, was almost the last exponent of the higher decency in international affairs.

Our final meeting was in 1931. Grey was in Northumberland, but came down to London for the reunion. We dined at the Oxford and Cambridge Club in Pall Mall. Through the meal the talk was all of birds and fish and Wordsworth's poetry, which the host could recite with apocalyptic emphasis. After the mutton and Burgundy were finished, we ascended to the third-floor library to smoke. There Grey took me to a window at the back, raised the blind, and said:

'I can't see them, but I suppose you can see lights over there across the park. They are the Houses of Parliament. Fifty years ago I came down from Northumberland to visit my uncle and see the play. He brought me here to dine as I have brought you. After dinner, he took me to this window, just as I have you. He pointed out those lights and said: "They are the Houses of Parliament." The Houses of Parliament, I said to myself. I wonder if I shall ever see the inside of them.'

He paused, and then, with brooding emotion, 'I sometimes wish I never had.'

The serene humor with which Edward Grey faced life was hardly won. Few men have taken more wicked blows from Fate. Dorothy, his first wife, was killed in a carriage accident after a few happy years; Pamela, Lady Glenconner, the congenial companion of his Indian Summer, lived but a few years after their late marriage; his favorite brother George, an African administrator, was killed by a lion, his brother Charles, seventeen years later, by a buffalo. He was a lover of his homes. Both of them, the old manor house of Fallodon and the fishing cottage on the Itchen at Winchester, were burned to the ground. The twenty-five years of his patient work for amity among nations ended in the battle smoke of a world war. In later years, failing sight shut him off from the finer techniques of his sport of fishing, made all the friendly birds that sat on his shoulder and took food from his hand look alike; made the last resource of reading impossible. Yet his spirit never faltered. Perhaps at heart he was sustained by an odd fatalistic adventuresomeness. When he was almost totally blind, it was a nerve-racking experience to walk with him on London streets. Without pausing for traffic stop or guidance, he would plunge across Piccadilly or Pall Mall as if they were the familiar trout rivers of Northumberland. Constables, when they saw him coming, would stop the traffic for a block.

It is always Edward Grey more than any other I have in mind when, in moments of doubt, anxiety, and depression, I say over to myself:

> What evil luck soever
> For me remains in store,
> 'Tis sure much finer fellows
> Have fared much worse before.

Not long after the war, with its near decimation of the white race, death for the first time threatened my own immediate family. After a series of heavy operations, my son, a boy of fourteen, developed a brain abscess. Hope was all but given up. His life was saved by a miracle of modern surgery. A technique just developed in the war hospitals in France made it possible to locate the invaded area with precision, and a brilliant brain operation pulled him through so completely that a few months later, with co-ordination and balance fully restored, he won the Junior National Championship at his sport of figure skating.

During his convalescence, Margaret MacDonald, the spectacled maid at Thayer's who had summoned Senator Lodge to the telephone to hear the terms of the armistice, was employed to read to him. Now for nearly a quarter of a century, Margaret and her sister, 'Mrs. Mac,' sometimes one, sometimes the other, sometimes both together, have supported the domestic front, with a competence and loyalty that have won gratitude and affection. I owe much to many rivers, but to none more than to Bear River North in Prince Edward's Island, whence they come.

One wonders whether, in that brave new world which is scheduled to follow the present war, we shall find similar companions to share our homes, and assist in the daily routines on which in the past what seemed the good life for both has been based.

CHAPTER 18

Dividend decade

AT A DINNER PARTY in London before the Old War, the talk turned on a certain noted figure in Threadneedle Street. 'He has,' said Hilaire Belloc, 'a gift of instant decision that has already lost him two fortunes and is now putting a third in jeopardy.' In the twenties, even the most instantaneous decisions which all the world was making could do you no harm. You put in your shoestring and pyramided it. Cash and stock dividends and profits poured in astronomically. While Calvin Coolidge, the safe and sane, was in the White House, and the money-changers in the temple, the market, like the skirts, seemed permanently on the up and up. One began to wonder whether even the sky was the limit.

In literature, too, the pot was boiling. In 1919, Joseph Hergesheimer, watching the boys coming home from France, wrote: 'Here was a most extraordinary and new audience, clear-eyed and critical, supremely invigorating, forever lost to the purely superficial.'

In 1922, I landed in New York from *The Old North State*, and successfully passed the customs with a bottle of Irish whiskey and a proof copy of James Joyce's *Ulysses*, which, at the suggestion of Havelock Ellis, I had procured from Sylvia

Beach at her shop in the Rue de l'Odéon. I had read it on shipboard, and while I didn't quite see myself proposing it for publication on Park Street, it was obvious that here was something that penetrated well below the purely superficial. I watched its fate in America with acute interest, and was amused and mad when Reed Smoot, on the floor of the United States Senate, that sounding board for the expression of the closed mind, shouted: 'It is written by a man with a diseased mind and a soul so black that he would even obscure the darkness of hell.' I noted how many of the better fictional manuscripts that came into the office began to show an awareness of the stream of consciousness. I breathed easier when John Woolsey of the Federal Circuit Court in New York, in phrases that revealed the poet and humanist as well as the judge, decided it was all right. 'The locale was Celtic and the season was spring.'

I had hoped that the house would be able to play its part in distributing the yeasty effervescence that was bubbling in our books as well as in our bathtubs. Slowly and painfully came the realization that it would be hard to do in Boston. Just how the town that had been for a century and a half the home of independent thought and free speech became the scene of the stiffest censorship of books is for the psycho-analysts to determine. The infantile exhibitionism of the vocabulary of many of the new writers was, no doubt, the spark that started the crusading fires of the Watch and Ward Society. Books were banned and not burnt, but the effect on the morale of Boston book trade was as bad. Booksellers could, and did, go to jail. If a Boston publisher's book had been suppressed, it might have been suppressed at the source, not, as when a New York book was 'banned in Boston,' supplied with a powerful pulling slogan for national advertising.

The Boston publishers, rather shamefacedly, played it safe.

After the death in 1926 of the reverend director of the Watch and Ward, the business of suppression was taken over by the booksellers themselves, in sensible liaison with the society; later by the police, and then the situation became really cockeyed. Most of the books that were withheld from the readers of Boston, except by bootleg mail order from New York, were no great cultural loss to them; but the suppression of books of the calibre of *Elmer Gantry, Black April, The Sun Also Rises, Manhattan Transfer,* and *An American Tragedy* was awkward for Boston publishers to explain to desirable authors in New York.

Toward the end of the trouble came the famous 'Hatrack' affair. Herbert Asbury had printed in Mencken's *Mercury* a touching, sombrely humorous story of a prostitute who conducted her business in a freight car on a siding back of a cemetery. She went penitently to church, but when refused salvation on her record, went back to the freight car. When the sale of that number became taboo in Boston, Mencken whooping joyfully came over to sell one in person on the historic Common. The night before I gave him a dinner at the St. Botolph Club — a sort of going-away-to-jail party; and next morning, watching from my window, saw my guest amidst a crowd of applauding spectators commit the overt act, and enter the Wagon for a ride. The case was dismissed by a wise judge, who thought that a person of sufficient intelligence to have acquired fifty cents and to be willing to spend it for a magazine of high literary quality, would not be menacingly inflamed by the reading of 'Hatrack.'

At the very end of the twenties, in the course of a review of Morris Ernst's *To the Pure,* I ventured to state the belief that, penny-catching pornography apart, impurity lies in the receiving mind; that the time may come when, just as in the Paris of that time, after street incidents, it was not the demon taxi-driver but the errant pedestrian that was arrested, so it will be not the offending volume but the offended reader that will be haled into court for an examination of his complexes.

Another deeper gulf between a Boston publisher and the authors of New York was the tragic case of Niccola Sacco, the shoe-worker, and Bartolomeo Vanzetti, the Emerson-reading fish-peddler. Emerson himself had noted in his 'Savings Bank,' on which we have already cashed one bearer check, that Transcendentalism was distrusted in State Street as tending to invalidate contracts. Now it was discovered it might even lead to murder.

Strange scenes were enacted behind the iron fence that bounds the Common facing my window. Edna Millay appeared and read a poem. As I recall it, the police were in the audience but didn't interfere. It would have taken a brave flat-foot to have laid a finger on that embodiment of blazing wrath. Dorothy Parker and John Dos Passos were less, or perhaps they considered themselves more, fortunate, and followed the John Bunyan trail to the police station.

In the last fifteen years, I have read the considerable body of literature the case has accumulated and reflected upon it. The more I read and reflect, the surer I feel that Vanzetti was innocent of the crime he was charged with, not quite so sure of Sacco. There was a difference in the weight of the evidence, and in the characters of the two defendants. Neither, I am convinced, would have been convicted in a legal and social atmosphere where it was possible for a reasonable doubt to raise its voice. In his Ingersoll Lecture at Harvard,

Lowes Dickinson inquired, 'Is immortality desirable?' I almost think it is, if only to get at the truth of the Sacco-Vanzetti case.

For these and other reasons, I found myself in the twenties a little out of tune with my Boston environment. Yet when the suggestion came that I might shift allegiance and take a partnership in a good house in my native New York, I could not, I found, brook the idea of forsaking Park Street, the Common, and the half-day's drive to New England mountains and rivers. A greater temptation came when invited to Washington, to edit the new *Dictionary of American Biography,* to be, as I phrased it in my mind, the American Leslie Stephen. But Washington I distrusted as a place to live. A capital that was not a metropolis, lacking the functions of industry and commerce, it seemed rather like a man with lungs and throat, perhaps a brain, but nothing whatever below the belt. Bacon had said we should treat the faults of our country, as of our natural parents, by kindly leading, not by contestation and reproach. Perhaps that was true of one's adopted city. I stayed put.

Although I failed to sign up some of the new American writers that gave me my own preferred reading, the business did well from the sale of competent and popular British authors that we had taken on during the War.

Anne Douglas Sedgwick, Mrs. Basil de Sélincourt, most successful of the group, would have been held higher by the new critics had her delicate art not fallen on a decade when stories of the upper middle class were considered 'Victorian' and inherently vicious. Born in Englewood, New Jersey, she was a *déracinée;* but she enjoyed the uprooted writer's advantages for the observation of national character and temperament. The contrasts of British and American *mores* in *Adrienne Toner,* of British and French in *The Little French Girl,* are less subtle and intricate than those of Henry James, but sharper and more dramatically employed.

With her prematurely white hair and lively blue eyes, Anne de Sélincourt suggested an old French miniature of some great and beautiful lady. Like all great ladies I have known, she was given to girlish giggles that were fascinating to provoke. I remember many walks with her in the fields of Kingham and shall never forget our last meeting, only a month or two before her death. She was in bed, more beautiful, more lively-eyed than ever. A paralysis of the throat had stilled her eager speech, and she could only communicate by paper and pencil. In earlier days we had talked of Wordsworth, as poet and man. News of his extra-territorial domestic life with Marie Anne Vallon in France had just been printed in America in a small book by Professor Harper of Princeton. I narrated the affair in some detail and affirmed that it made me understand Wordsworth better, and like him more, both as man and poet. Anne seized her pad and scribbled her agreement, with embellishing comment. For the twenty minutes I was allowed to see her, tongue and pencil dealt with the affair in all its bearings. Her scribbles were witty as well as wise. It was heart-breaking, but it was bravely inspiring. At the end of my allotted twenty minutes, I took last leave, feeling more poignantly than ever that she was a very great lady.

There was more of the fierce fighting spirit in Georges Clemenceau than in any other man I ever encountered. In the later half of the dividend decade, a contract had been signed with the Tiger for a sort of *Summa* like that of Saint

Thomas Aquinas, a survey and synthesis of all knowledge. It was hoped that it would be made concrete and readable by illustrations from the events of the author's remarkable life, and enlivened by flashes of his celebrated wit. When the French manuscript came in, that hope was dashed. But a contract was a contract, and Clemenceau was a good name. Charles Miner Thompson was engaged to supply a translation. When it was finally published, Clemenceau co-operatively died the day before its appearance in the bookstores. In two stout volumes, at a high price, it had a helpful sale. No one has ever been found who read it through, though the smarter reviewers discovered the eloquent paragraphs that loom through its prismatic mist.

Thompson had found its fifteen hundred pages hard going and publication had been delayed from season to season. Fierce letters began coming from the Tiger demanding action. Finding myself in Paris, I mustered the courage to call on the indignant author. Clemenceau, who breakfasted on onion soup and carrots at sunrise, appointed the hour of eight-thirty. Punctually I arrived at an apartment on the ground floor in the Rue Franklin and was told to wait in a very strange room. Perhaps sixteen feet square, it had in its middle a raised platform so large that it left only two or three feet of space around it. The platform was occupied by an enormous circular desk, into which one entered, closing a swinging door behind him. The high mesa of the desk was covered with ivory elephants, Sphinxes, and Buddhas, symbols of the thought of the brooding East, where their owner had gone for peace after Versailles. It was obvious that the caller occupying a straight, hard chair on the lower level was in about as commanding a position as a pupil before the teacher, or a culprit before the judge.

Presently there were excursions and alarums and the strangest of figures entered. The face of the ex-Premier of France needs no description, but it had to be seen in full color to be appreciated. His complexion was of a dark ruby red, his eyes like coals just ready to burst into flame. His costume missed making him a figure of fun by enough margin to leave him rather terrible — a black sack suit of superior quality, on his head a poilu's cap of horizon blue, on his hands grey gloves, on his feet huge grey footwarmers that suggested one of his elephants. When he entered his desk and was seen from below, only from the waist up, he seemed the biggest of the Buddhas.

After the briefest of salutations, he launched a torrent of French, scolding his visitor for needless delay in the appearance of his book. Remembering the author's early years in New York, I tried to shift the conversation into English. The Tiger would have none of that, and, more fiercely than ever, continued in his own tongue. I braced myself and joined in, not doing too well, but well enough to check the flood and to make a firm statement of progress. I ventured a feeble French wise-crack that brought what might have been a faint chuckle from on high. After a half-hour of miscellaneous conversation, chiefly on the German character of which Clemenceau held a low view, we parted politely, even amicably.

On the way back to the Boulevard Raspail I stopped at one of the bookshops to be found in every block of the Paris of that day, and bought what I should have read the day before, a small volume entitled *L'Esprit de Clemenceau,* two hundred pages of anecdotes and quoted epigrams that deserve more attention from anthologists than they have received. The epigrams are wicked, the anecdotes revealing. Back in the Revolution of 1870, during an important debate the eloquent voice of Clemenceau, scheduled to speak following Gambetta, was not heard. He was searched for, and found at an auction sale of *objets,* but refused to return. After the debate was over, he appeared in the Chamber and, carefully extracting numerous charming cups and saucers from capacious pockets, remarked: 'Ce qu'il y a de plus difficile dans une révolution c'est de préserver la porcelaine.'

Near the end of his life, he said: 'La suprême vertu est la patience de vivre.'

While the twenties were the Augustan age of the house for the publication of successful books from England and the Continent, they were by no means barren of hopeful writers at home. Two first novels won Pulitzer prizes, Margaret Barnes's *Years of Grace* and Oliver La Farge's *Laughing Boy*. Esther Forbes for the first half of the decade sat in the next room reading manuscripts, with an uncommon flair for the new real thing. Her own new real thing, *O Genteel Lady!* was one of the first books of fiction sent out by the new Book of the Month Club, to the little-acorn tune of fourteen thousand copies.

Now that the book clubs' business has grown to a great oak, with distributions of a quarter of a million or more, there has been some uneasiness lest the focussing of the literary limelight on a small group of fortunate books to the exclusion of others of equal merit might be harmful. Twenty years ago, the 'six best-sellers' judged by any critical standard were a job lot of books. Now the two major clubs send out some four hundred thousand volumes each month — five million copies of twenty-four titles a year. They are chosen by persons of wide human interests, who are writers themselves, who know quality and interest when they see it in proof. I believe the circulation of those five million well-chosen volumes every year has made it possible for a book of quality today, even if not sent out by a club, to attract a public at least double that it could have won in the early twenties.

Looking back over the dividend decade as a whole, I like it less than any other. I had a good time, and good fishing at home, in Ireland, in England, and in France. I became, too, better acquainted with indoor sports; the partnership pleasures of bridge, the deep strategy of dominoes, the duello or gang warfare of backgammon. But the catch of authors included none that seemed likely to exhibit the literary longevity of Willa Cather or Henry Adams.

A little before the *débâcle* of 1929, I converted certain inflated securities into land in the ancient town of Ipswich, an old house, two barns, and numerous outhouses that at least couldn't fly out of the window. The mellow countryside lacks the grave beauty of the Lake or the White Hills, but the rolling dunes have a potent charm. History is there too. In Ipswich, Ann Bradstreet was writing verse while Charles the First was King of Massachusetts, and across the low slope of Wilderness Hill I see the small bare house Sergeant Low, ancester of the founder of my own former Low Fellowship, left for the capture of Louisburg in 1745. Every summer into the sounds, estuaries, and salt creeks comes the mysterious migration of the sporting striped bass.

At the end of that bountiful and damned decade my frame of mind was rather that of the ancient Chinese scholar

Chuangtse, expounder of Tao and the rhythm of life, as reported by Lin Yutang:

'Chuangtse was fishing on the P'u River when the Prince of Ch'u sent two high officials to see him and said, "Our Prince desires to burden you with the administration of the Ch'u State." Chuangtse went on fishing without turning his head and said, "I have heard that in Ch'u there is a sacred tortoise which died when it was three thousand years old. The Prince keeps this tortoise carefully enclosed in a chest in his ancestral temple. Now would this tortoise rather be dead and have its remains venerated, or would it rather be alive and wagging its tail in the mud?"

' "It would rather be alive," replied the two officials, "and wagging its tail in the mud."

' "Begone!" cried Chuangtse. "I too will wag my tail in the mud." '

But for me the ironic gods had other plans.

Part Five

CHAPTER 19

Laocoön,
or fighting the percentages

THE IMPACT OF THE DEPRESSION beginning in the autumn of '29 and getting harder for three successive years had strange by-products. Panhandlers thronged the Common, as numerous and noisy as the starlings. They started from all directions when they saw me coming, swinging the stick. I found that if, instead, I leaned heavily on it and exhibited a slight limp they were diverted from the attack. About the time of the presidential election of 1932, a new note was struck in American photographic portraiture. Our leaders were depicted showing not a frowning, statesmanlike gravity, but all their teeth, as if caught in the act of roaring with laughter at some Rabelaisian anecdote or slap-stick farce. This depressed me still further.

During the Old War, I had been added to the executive committee of the company and in the twenties became involved more in the business, less in the literary aspect of publishing. In March, 1933, the month all the banks took a holiday and some of them folded up, I undertook the general management of the trade business.

The classic group of Laocoön and his sons tangling with serpents, that Lessing made the basis for his analysis of the arts, is a fair representation of what modern accounting has done to a publisher. In the good old days, he took in as much as he could collect and paid out as little. If, at the end of the month or year, there was still cash in the till, that was profit and expendable. Now he fights a daily skirmish with mathematical curves and never knows the outcome till the end of his fiscal year. Sinuous percentages coil round him, *spirisque ligant ingentibus:* gross sales, net sales, serial sales, foreign sales, copyright sales, plate rentals, film sales, other trading income; cost of sales, commissions paid, depreciation, cash discounts, royalties, plates, selling, advertising, administration, reserves for bad debts. He finds that keeping the poisonous ones down, so far from fattening the benign ones up, not infrequently thins them to emaciation. The war is fought out over yellow monthly sheets containing six columns of figures of fifty items each, sometimes spotted with an eruption of red. Every figure can represent the patient reconciliation of opposing schools of thought, decisions affecting the lives of men and their families, the cautious achieving of the equilibrium of the heterogeneous.

There seem not to be enough hours in the day to do what must be done. As Confucius said, stating the obvious five hundred years before Christ, the desire to have things done quickly prevents their being done thoroughly. One fights that natural desire along with the percentages; leading the unleadable, answering the unanswerable. Any decision is not always better than none. Sometimes the dossier that is allowed to sink to the bottom of the agenda basket settles itself, as Nature spreads the soft concealing grass over the harrowed battlefield.

The administration of a trade publishing business is a tough job, but not the least fascinating of indoor sports.

With loyal and able assistance, I survived and saw it through for nine years, but my extra-curricular reading was confined to fishing books and murder stories.

In 1933, a new name appeared in the catalogue that listed Emerson and Longfellow, Lord Grey and Calvin Coolidge and Clemenceau — that of Adolf Hitler. In *Pan Germanism,* published a year before the Old War, the publishers had a conscious scoop. In *My Battle*, the shortened version of *Mein Kampf,* they knew they had something, but not quite what. They had seen pictures of a little man looking like Charlie Chaplin, who had been in the hoosegow, and then, no one seemed to know quite why or how, had become Chancellor of the German Empire; taking over the controls of government from good old Hindenburg, the former personification of Prussian frightfulness, of whom the Anglo-Saxon public was becoming rather fond. They learned that this Hitler, or Schicklgruber, or whatever his funny name was, now the actual head of a great state, had written while in prison an eccentric book in two volumes called *Mein Kampf,* setting forth the story of his life, his views on government, his ideas for the future of the German people. It appeared to be something that should be looked into. They did so by cable and letter and, within a few months, arranged for and published a streamlined version in English by Captain E. T. S. Dugdale, grandnephew of Lord Macaulay.

Captain Dugdale did a sound job. He made the book a little more coherent, a shade less extravagant than the original, but, though he brought it down to a size the British and American publics could be expected to buy and read, omitted none of the leading ideas or pronouncements of policy and intention. Its publication was attended by storm clouds and electrical disturbances over Park Street. One school of thought was outraged that the book had been published at all, another that it had not been published in its entirety. As the intentions foreshadowed in *Mein Kampf* were put progressively into action, the latter step came to be both possible and desirable. It was taken, and the present wide distribution of the book in English is now perhaps its own most effective counter-propaganda. It is one of the pleasantest great ironies of history that the legal decisions sustaining the American copyright have protected their literary properties and given security to the German thinkers and writers who fled from Hitler for their lives.

It had been maintained by the opposition that Hitler, at the time the book was published, was neither an Austrian nor a German, but a 'stateless person' and not entitled to enjoy the protection of United States copyright. The learned judges held that one had but to be a citizen of the world, if the formalities were duly observed, to have the usufruct of the products of his brains secured to him by the copyright law of this country.

It was said long ago that only children and fools tell their dreams. It is more foolish than ever, now that the simplest objects in the world of dreams have been given the most lurid symbolisms. You suddenly find some student of Freud leering at you with evil comprehension of your complexes. Yet I will take a chance.

Early in 1940, during the period of the 'phony' war, the strategy of terror, and the progress of *Mein Kampf* through the federal courts, I had one of my habitual current-events dreams. I was called up, as it seemed, by Dr. Gustave Müller, the German Consul-General in New York. Did I understand the German language? I replied that I did, had studied it for three years in school and college, had found occasion to read it extensively while working in the University for a doctoral degree, still tackled manuscripts in German when no one else could be found to do it, and frequently picked up the *Lieder* of Heine and the *Sonnets* and *Elegies* of Rilke.

Dr. Müller said, 'Es macht mir Freude.' (O doctor!) Der Fuehrer had just notified him that he was flying to America to make an important proposal to the people of the United States, and instructed him to assemble a large but carefully chosen dinner party of the best minds to receive it. Would I turn up at the Plaza Hotel in New York Monday week at eight? White tie. Piqued and flattered, I replied: 'Jawohl.'

Arriving at the Plaza exactly on time, punctuality is the politeness of princes, I was directed, not into the hotel itself, but across Fifty-Ninth Street to an ornate pavilion that had been erected in the Park alongside the statue of General Sherman, preceded by the Angel of Peace. Entering, I found myself in an anteroom, amid a numerous company all in tails. I recognized and had passing conversation with William Allen White, Felix Frankfurter, Archibald MacLeish, Ellery Sedgwick, Elmer Davis, two fellow directors from Park Street, the able legal adviser who was conducting our copyright case, and Curtice Hitchcock, who had co-operated in the publication of the complete edition. After a flourish of Wagnerian music, which seemed to come from a double quartette of trombones, folding doors were flung open and we were ushered into a second apartment, which seemed to be a sort of Rathskeller. At a high table, bemedalled and majestic, sat Goebbels and Goering. Between them was an empty chair of papal magnificence, a swastika embroidered upon its velvet back.

After a barrage of Heil Hitlers, word was passed that Der

Fuehrer had been delayed, and we were invited to be seated and partake of refreshment. Waiters appeared offering large steins with choice of Pilsener or Muenchener, accompanied by pretzels, frankfurters, and wiener-schnitzel. A long wait ensued. There was some half-hearted singing of *Ach, du lieber Augustin,* and *Mein Schatz ist ein Ritter;* but the affair was becoming tedious.

Suddenly a malaise invaded the guests, the pavilion began to vibrate, there was a sense of levitation, the waiters threw off their aprons and became storm troopers with nasty-looking Lügers. The pavilion was a Zeppelin, bound for a concentration camp somewhere behind the Siegfried Line. The best minds had been kidnapped!

Pierced with the thought of the anxiety of my family, I awoke bedewed with chilly sweat.

Harrowing as my dreams sometimes are, I would not give them up. They add variety to *la vie,* and make going to sleep always an adventure. One wonders whether Alph, the sacred river, was not for Coleridge a symbol of consciousness when it ran

> Through caverns measureless to man
> Down to a sunless sea.

During the decade of the thirties, entanglement in percentages, and dealings with native authors kept me more at home, and I made but three journeys overseas. On one of these an acquaintance with two diversely eminent Englishmen teased my mind to a Plutarchian comparison of their senses of humor; Stanley Baldwin, head of the British government for fifteen years, now Earl Baldwin of Bewdley, and Havelock Ellis, psychologist of sex.

At breakfast at 10 Downing Street, early in 1937, I sat

opposite the shrewd, rugged, humorous face of 'Bumbling' Baldwin and perceived at once that the adjective could not possibly be other than the *mot injuste*. I have no admiration for the 'men of Munich,' and believe that history will disassociate Stanley Baldwin from them. After breakfast, the Prime Minister filled a cherry-wood pipe with American cut-plug tobacco from a familiar olive-green box with a red circle on it, and announced that he had smoked little else since it had been introduced to him by Charles Eliot Norton while visiting at Shady Hill forty years before. By the time the pipe was finished, we had exchanged information on Boston and Cambridge in the gay nineties, together with views on the recent royal marriage, and I learned something of the poetry-loving, nature-loving, truth-loving mind of my interlocutor, his basic good will and never-failing humor.

Two years later, as fellow guests at Government House in Ottawa, we smoked other pipes together and I divined more of the art of governing men by understanding and tact, arriving at your own ends by other people's means; 'by those personal qualities,' as Lord Grey wrote him, 'that can be summed up as the gift of making troubles better and not worse.' How else had Stanley Baldwin dealt with the general strike of 1926, or begun to re-establish the British Air Force four years before Munich, in the face of a dissenting Parliament and an indifferent country? It is recorded that one day, when Parliament had been unusually difficult and the results of an important division seemed in doubt, he whispered in the ear of the Chancellor of the Exchequer at his side: 'I met a drover forty years ago, having trouble getting his pigs along the road to market. I asked him how he was doing. He said, "A hard thing to drive many on 'em, very, is a pig." '

One evening at Rideau Hall, the Ladies Baldwin and Tweedsmuir were telling of the induction of their husbands to chieftainships in Canadian Indian tribes. Said charmingly Victorian Lady Baldwin, 'And do you know what Stanley did when they put that big feathered thing on his head? He turned to me and said, "Now you are my squaw!" '

No man of my acquaintance had less of the true spirit of humor than Havelock Ellis. At first you were deceived by his constant smile and frequent laughter, but you soon saw that this came, not along with anything really amusing, but in recognition of some happy idea or well-chosen word, yours or his; that it was an agreeable nervous habit. In the seven volumes of his *Psychology of Sex,* there is never a twinkle. Perhaps a man with a real sense of humor couldn't or wouldn't have written seven volumes on that solemn subject. Yet an occasional hint of a perception of the incongruous that is not infrequently there might have made its effect more rather than less scientific.

An eminent Boston physician in his will left his set of the *Psychology* to the library of the club called after the Lincolnshire saint. One by one, the volumes disappeared from the shelves. At the end of three months, all were gone. Whether at the hands of curious youth or reminiscent age was never ascertained. *Si jeunesse savait; si vieillesse pouvait!*

It was, no doubt, the absence of humor from his composition that kept Ellis's most ambitious case history, his own *My Life,* from standing, as he hoped and believed it would, beside the *Confessions* of Saint Augustine and Rousseau. Neither of these is a book for laughter, but humor, or the sense of proportion, which is the same thing, went into their making. *My Life* is a completer self-revelation than either, but less typically important and historically significant. Its minutely documented record of a tragically unsuccessful modern marriage, coming from the philosopher of love and psychologist of sex, has a breath-taking irony. I never suggested that the title be changed to one I had been keeping in the back of my mind against just such an occasion — *Sailors Can't Swim*. To me, remembering both the buoyant author of *The Dance of Life* and the rosy, blue-eyed, curly-headed small woman whose plays I also published, it is quite the saddest book in the world.

As the belt-tightened thirties slipped by, publishable manuscripts found a sellers' market. Competition was keener, particularly at home. Before 1914, a publishing venturer returning from abroad came from a riper to a rawer land. In the twenties, the centre of gravity — industrial, economic, financial, even cultural — seemed to be moving westward. How many great novelists and poets were lying mute in the fields of Flanders we shall never know. Whatever the cause, more serious fiction was being written on the western shore of the Atlantic. By the mid-thirties, instead of all American publishers sailing once every year, sometimes twice, for London, there was a parade of their British colleagues to New York and Boston. It is reported that in 1942, twenty-seven per cent of the new books published in Britain were of American origin.

Through the depressed years, the quality of the three thousand manuscripts annually submitted to Park Street improved. Trouble seemed to make people think, to try to discover causes and cures. It quickened all their mental processes. Faced with adversity and sharper competition, authors wrote harder, and some of them pruned more. The

Fellowships, established to make possible the completion of promising work in progress, discovered new young authors of distinction. American literature is again on the march. Compare the books of today with those of *New England: Indian Summer,* even with those of the *Flowering.* Read *The Grapes of Wrath* after *The Rise of Silas Lapham,* even after *The House of Seven Gables,* or the criticism of Wilson, Mumford, Brooks, Canby, Fadiman, Krutch, or young Alfred Kazin after that of E. P. Whipple, T. W. Higginson, even Lowell. In humanity, insight, and imagination, our writers have grown with the country. They have achieved a new, a true, a riper humanism, and they are writing for a public that has multiplied ten, perhaps a hundredfold.

There is no living historian as yet whom I prefer to Parkman, with his matchless industry and genius for style, but in professional competence and readability, there are a dozen I would put only a little lower. The secondary list-fillers of today — biographies, topical books, reportage — are on a higher plane of literary ability than they have ever been before.

The defeatist fear that motion picture and radio would be the death of literature has proved baseless. After this New War, when the young men come home from the stratosphere and from under the seas, in every corner of the habitable or uninhabitable globe, there will be another new audience in the United States, and in all the British Commonwealth of Nations as well, more supremely invigorating than before. We shall have, I believe, writers who can give those clear-eyed critical readers the kind of books, in infinite variety, they will want. Perhaps a global war will be followed by a global literature in the English tongue. It is an intriguing thought for publishers as well as readers. *Qui vivra verra!*

CHAPTER 20

Portrait of a friend

IN WRITING of his fishing friend, Sir Henry Wotton, poet and ambassador, Izaak Walton took out of my mouth words I would apply to my own friend, John Buchan: 'A man with whom I have often fished and conversed, a man whose foreign employments in the service of his nation, a man whose experience, learning, wit, and cheerfulness made his company to be esteemed one of the delights of mankind.'

During the war and the first years of 'peace,' our meetings were in London, hurried, a little hectic, with no time for the reflective pause in the rapid fire of conversation. We tired the sun with talking and sent him down the sky. With the twenties, the scene changed to the more leisurely Cotswolds. A country boy, walker of hills and wader of streams, John had felt the life of town and trench, which was his in the war, made harder, not easier, by 'the scent of hawthorn and lilac battling with the stink of poison gas, and bird song in the pauses of the great guns.' Soon after the war was over, he sold his commodious house in Portland Place and, after considering an Elizabethan residence on a productive stretch of the Coln at Bibury, found his perfect setting four miles from Oxford in the little Manor House of Elsfield, by the Cherwell. It was not unlike that happy bird-haunted retreat in which Sir Richard Hannay is discovered in the opening chapters of *The Three Hostages*.

Like Henry James's in Rye, the hospitable front door opened directly from the village street; at Elsfield it was set in stonework of Saxon construction. At the back, one looked over a walled garden down sloping shaded fields to the slow Cherwell, where coarse fish passed their sleepy lives unmolested by the fly-fishing lord of the Manor. In the middle distance was a gazebo where Samuel Johnson liked to come for tea and talk with his friend Francis Wise, librarian of the Radcliffe. To the far left were visible the dreaming spires of Oxford — Saint Mary's, the Magdalen, and Christ Church towers, the dome of the Radcliffe Camera.

Within the house, the tradition of talk was more honored in the observance than in the breach. During weekends at Elsfield, in the course of long tramps through pastures, by spinneys and ancient woods, always in winter or early spring, when the primal forms of the land were bare, and we got the essential savor of earth and wood and water, exchanging experiences, and views on books and men, our friendship became consolidated and assured.

Bacon tells us that talking makes a ready man, but reading a full man. Back of John's ready utterance was a mind full to overflowing. In a paper on Sir Walter Scott, he has himself recorded what else he did during the three weeks in bed during the Old War, when I found him doing those four things at once:

'In the spring of 1917,' he writes, 'I was compelled, for reasons not unconnected with public affairs, to spend a considerable time in bed, and, in the pleasant idle weeks of convalescence, I amused myself with carrying out a plan which

I had long contemplated. I had been in the habit of reading some of the Waverley Novels every year, but on this occasion I re-read carefully what I considered the best — *Waverley, Old Mortality, Guy Mannering, The Antiquary, Rob Roy, The Bride of Lammermoor, The Heart of Midlothian,* and *Redgauntlet.* Then I read my favorites among the voluminous works of Alexandre Dumas, the Valois and D'Artagnan cycles; then Victor Hugo's *Notre Dame* and *Les Misérables;* and I concluded with half a dozen of Balzac.'

The opportunity was special, but the achievement not, for him, exceptional. He was a swift, omnivorous reader, but never so hasty as to miss any telling phrase or micrometric *nuance.* He read the best of the current novels, English and American, biography, poetry, travel, philosophy, always a little Latin or Greek, and deeply in the fields of his special interests, Scottish and English history and the American Civil War.

He wrote as rapidly as he read. In the quarter century of our dealings as author and publisher, forty titles, running to more than fifty volumes, appeared on the Park Street list. It was during the war and the first years at Elsfield that he wrote the sterling novels of adventure for which he is best known to the wider public. Many of them were set down on a pad held on his knees during the daily round trip of three hours between Oxford and the publishing offices of Thomas Nelson's Sons in the shadow of Saint Paul's. He referred to them lightly as his 'shilling shockers,' but one has only to compare them with the numerous tales described as 'in the manner of Buchan' to see their individuality and pre-eminence. From *The Thirty-Nine Steps,* written in the early days of the War, through all the doings of Richard Hannay and his fellow adventurers of the Runagates Club, they strike a note of poetry and high courage that set them above other contemporary work in the field. What he said in *Pilgrim's Way* of Basil Blackwood is true of any of his heroes: 'He was of the same breed as the slender gallants who singed the beard of the King of Spain and, like Essex, tossed their plumed hats into the sea in joy of the enterprise, or who sold their swords to whatever cause had daylight and honour in it. His like had left their bones in farther places than any race on earth, and from their uncharted wanderings our empire was born.'

The tales were never artfully contrived, and subtlely phrased, fifteen hundred words a day, like Stevenson's before the Vailima days when he took to dictation. Buchan never invented with the pen in his hand; he waited until the story had told itself to him, and then, like his master Scott, poured it out in his swift, small, all but illegible hand. It pleased him and his most devoted reader that in the pursuits and hurried journeys that fill these books, there is always a trout or salmon river to be followed, a mountain to be climbed.

In 1924, John and Susan Buchan paid a visit to the States. I drove them around New Hampshire, which reminded them of the Highlands of Scotland. We climbed Chocorua, and John, another member of the Alpine Club, proved an even more testing companion of the trail than Trevelyan had been. Talking continuously, even on the steepest stretches, he accomplished the ascent in fifty minutes. Foaming at the mouth, but trying to look pleasant, I just managed to keep within sound of the one-sided conversation.

We went to Washington, where I sat in the outer office of the White House talking with C. Bascom Slemp, while John went in to see President Coolidge. He came out after an hour, twice his allotted time, flushed and smiling. Asked what they had been talking about, he replied, 'Latin poetry.' The President, he said, had shown a surprising knowledge of Virgil and Horace, and had spoken eloquently of what the language and literature of Rome had meant to him all his life.

I inquired, rather sceptically, 'Wasn't it you that were doing most of the talking?'

'No,' he said, 'it was the President himself.'

From Washington, we set out in a large open car for a ten days' tour of the battlefields of Virginia, where, as Mary Johnston told us later, when we stopped with her overnight at Three Hills, the trunks of trees are so full of bullets that sawmill accidents are of daily occurrence.

We drove through the fat fields of Maryland to Antietam and Harper's Ferry, and up the valley of the Shenandoah. Equipped with old Confederate battle maps, we followed the marching and counter-marching of Stonewall Jackson's Valley campaign. At Port Republic, we approached a house marked on the map 'Lewis House,' and found old Miss Lewis sitting on the piazza where she had sat, a young girl, on a June day in 1862, and seen Wheat's Tigers of Taylor's Louisiana Brigade burst from the woods back of the house to capture a Massachusetts battery on its front.

To my Brady and Frank Leslie's-own-artist-in-the-field-fed imagination, the Valley Pike and the wood roads that climb through the gaps of the Blue Ridge and the Massanuttens were thronged with thin, bearded men in shabby grey uniforms. But it was John who told us, told even Sam Morison, who had joined us at Washington, the names of the mountains without looking at the map.

From Staunton, we drove to Charlottesville, pausing at 'Miramar' for a glass of Langhorne Madeira; then on to

Richmond, and under the expert guidance of Douglas Freeman, covered the terrain of the Seven Days, from the Chickahominy to Malvern Hill. There John decided to leave to Freeman the biography of Lee on the scale of Henderson's *Stonewall Jackson,* that he had long planned to undertake. We visited the great houses along the James, Westover, and Shirley, and turned north again through Fredericksburg to Washington. John's memory of the trip through the perspective of fifteen years was set down in a paragraph of the eloquent chapter in *Pilgrim's Way* entitled 'My America':

'I came first into the United States by way of Canada — a good way to enter, for English eyes are already habituated to the shagginess of the landscape and can begin to realize its beauties. My first reflection was that no one had told me how lovely the country was. I mean lovely, not vast or magnificent. I am not thinking of the Grand Canyon and the Yosemite and the Pacific coast, but of the ordinary rural landscape. There is much of the land which I have not seen, but in the East and the South and the Northwest I have collected a gallery of delectable pictures. I think of the farms which are clearings in the Vermont and New Hampshire hills, the flowery summer meadows, the lush cow-pastures with an occasional stump to remind one that it is old forest land, the quiet lakes and the singing streams, the friendly accessible mountains; the little country towns of Massachusetts and Connecticut with their village greens and elms and two-century-old churches and courthouses; the secret glens of the Adirondacks and the mountain meadows of the Blue Ridge; the long-settled champaign of Maryland and Pennsylvania; Virginian manors more Old-England perhaps than anything we have at home; the exquisite links with the past like much of Boston and Charleston and all of Annapolis.'

It was during this visit that, for the first time, I heard him make a public speech. I was astounded and charmed when the quiet, swift voice to which I was accustomed deepened its pitch and increased its volume, taking on old cadences of the Kirk of Scotland, and an eloquence I had not heard since the brief church-going period of my own youth.

A frequent topic of conversation during the weeks we were together was the part field sports shared might play in international understanding. A little later, the manuscript of a new novel, *Courts of the Morning*, came over from him with a summarizing dedication to me in verse:

> The same old tremor of the spring
> Assails the heart of you and me;
> Nor does the reel less blithely ring
> By Willowemoc than by Dee.

> As bright the Ammonoosuc streams
> Dance through their silent scented woods
> As those which fill my waking dreams
> In Hebridean solitudes.

> Your land, old friend, is one with mine,
> Whate'er may hap from time or tide,
> While, with St. Izaak the Divine,
> We worship at the waterside.

In acknowledging it I quoted Thoreau's fine saying, 'The stars are apexes of what triangles!'

The following spring, we had a week together, harling for spring salmon in the picturesque stretch of the Tay known as the Meiklelour Water from the charming manor of that name. There I learned that he was planning to give up his active partnership in the prosperous Nelson business, and go in for Parliament and politics, where was still to be found a Briton's greatest, most honorable, and endless adventure. He was elected by a large majority as the member for the Scottish Universities — Saint Andrews, Glasgow, Aberdeen, and Edinburgh — as if all the New England colleges were to get together and send a single representative to Congress. It proved a loyal and well-satisfied constituency.

After his entrance to Parliament, a graver note came into his writing. The adventure stories skirted nearer the edge of tragedy, and the historical novels, *Witchwood* and *The Blanket of the Dark*, were his most serious fictions. He had the two best gifts for the historical novelist, the love of place and the sense of wonder. In *Witchwood*, it was the border country of the Tweed, where he had spent the long summers of his youth; in *The Blanket of the Dark* the Cotswolds between the valleys of the Windrush and the Evenlode, where in his prime he took his forty-mile walks. Through both the horns of Elfland blow. In these stories, as in his biographies of Montrose and Cromwell, he seemed to have conquered time and become the contemporary of the three hundred years of British history of which he wrote. He was pleased and startled when I quoted to him, with a *tu quoque,* the limerick about the remarkable Miss Bright,

> Who could travel more swiftly than light,
> Took a walk one day,
> In a relative way,
> And returned on the previous night.

Toward the end of his eight years in Parliament, he came to occupy a peculiar position of triangular liaison between the two elements of the National Government and the Crown. All three valued his historical learning, his Scottish good sense and discretion, his human touch. Many days he would breakfast with Ramsay MacDonald, circle the duck ponds in St. James's Park with Stanley Baldwin, and lunch at Buckingham Palace with 'The People's King,' about whom he was to write one of his best books, more fulfilled than any other with the rhythms of *The Pilgrim's Progress* that had entranced his boyish ear on Sunday afternoons in the little grey manse by the Fife shore.

In 1934, he confided that pro-consular duties and honors were impending. Next year he wrote that he had been appointed Governor-General to Canada, that he had been raised to the peerage, and had selected as his 'alias for parties' the title of Lord Tweedsmuir, the name of the little village on the Border that stood in his mind for his happiest memories. He said I would understand. I replied that I did. That if I were ever raised to an American peerage, I would choose to be none other than Lord Saint-Sacrement.

No post could have suited Lord Tweedsmuir better than Ottawa, no other could have better suited the post. He knew his Parkman and the writings of the Abbé Casgrain by heart; no earlier Governor-General had ever been in imagination so much the contemporary of the whole course of Canadian history, in temperament so completely the *voyageur.* His westward passage up the narrowing St. Lawrence and his landing under the shadows on the Rock were, he said, the most thrilling days of his life. During the first years, while his health and that of the world permitted, he visited every corner of the Dominion, by special train, by airplane to the frozen north, by canoe down virgin rivers. Thousands of square miles of wilderness became a park bearing his name. He made quite literally a million friends. When I went to Ottawa, the week of his death, porters, conductors, small shopkeepers, men in the street, spoke of him with broken voices. Even the French press of separatist Quebec, which had greeted his arrival with epithets of *agent provocateur* and *espion,* spoke of him with remorseful eloquence.

With his sense of its historic symbolism, he came to take an amused pleasure in the vice-regal etiquette that was observed at Rideau Hall and at the Citadel in Quebec. He never came through an open door. It was closed, then opened by an aide announcing 'His Excellency.' Off parade, it was 'His Ex.'

Not until the spring of 1938 were 'His Ex' and I able to fish again together. Then, occupying the luxurious lodge of an overlord of the lumber industry, we had a short week on the Montmorency. No river can be more lovely. The configuration of the Laurentian Mountains north of Quebec is such that, looking up a long stretch of any stream, one sees a succession of bold promontories, smaller Anthony's Noses, that give it the look of the Vale of Tempe. The slow curves of the Montmorency were precisely right to produce the effect to perfection. In every curve was a stretch of fruitful dry-fly water, with a better than pound average. In the confluent Rivière des Neiges, descending through an awesome series of Devil's Punch Bowls and Diana's Baths, the fish were fewer but bigger.

Good as the fishing was, the talk was better. One evening we returned to the juicy subject of debate we had argued since 1917. Had the internal combustion engine done the world more harm than good? I had always held for harm.

It had, I maintained, been a disturber of the world's peace, bad for the fishing. It had made our knowledge of place more extensive, perhaps, but less intensive. Kenneth Roberts had told me that, in preparing for a chapter of his *Northwest Passage,* he had spent three days motoring through the country between Lake Memphremagog and the Connecticut River. Parkman, in a note to *Montcalm and Wolfe,* says he had spent some weeks walking through the same terrain. Locomotion had taken the place of meditation. By providing the mechanical medium of swift attack and aggression on land, in the air, on and under the sea, it had been and would continue to be the cause of world wars.

After an enumeration of instances on both sides, lasting through the evening, I surrendered to the conclusion more formally stated two years later in *Pilgrim's Way:*

'If a man so dominates a machine that it becomes a part of him, he may thereby pass out of a narrow world to an ampler ether. The true airman is one of the freest of God's creatures, for he has used a machine to carry him beyond the pale of the Machine. He is a creator and not a mechanic, a master and not a slave.'

But the thoughts that chiefly occupied His Ex's mind, both on the Montmorency and back on the terrace of the Citadel, were of Anglo-American friendship and co-operation. One day he disclosed his thought that a visit of their Britannic majesties, George and Elizabeth, to both their Dominion of Canada and their friends of the United States would be helpful. Another day he ventured the proposition that the kinship of the English and American peoples was evidenced in the fact that the phrase 'a good man' meant the same thing to both, quite other than its meaning to French or Italian or German. Three weeks later, in Washington, he expressed the idea more fully in an impromptu speech to the two houses of Congress.

My last visit was in Ottawa in 1939. I came away gravely anxious. The malady that for a quarter of a century had beset the slight body that housed that valiant spirit had grown worse. The Governor-General went through the exhausting routine of his work, but at what cost of dogged nervous effort! Then came the War. He wrote, 'We are entering a long dark tunnel, but I believe there is light at the end.' He carried on the vice-regal round more splendidly than ever. Some of his best speeches were made in the open air to troops, in sleet or snow, on cold winter mornings. As usual he was writing three books at the same time, his 'Essay in Recollection,' *Pilgrim's Way;* his perhaps even more autobiographic last adventure story, *Mountain Meadow,* first entitled and still called in England, *Sick Heart River;* his book of Canadian legends for young readers. The completed manuscript of the first reached me late in January, 1940. Two weeks later came the report of his sudden illness. The news was better, worse, better again. Then came the voice of Elmer Davis at the close of his evening communiqué: 'Lord Tweedsmuir died tonight at seven-thirty.'

At Ottawa, a few days later, I was given the autograph manuscript of two unfinished chapters of *Pilgrim's Rest,* the fishing book he had begun immediately upon finishing *Pilgrim's Way.* Deciphering with difficulty the cursive script, I read the last words that came from that tireless pen. It was the conclusion of an excursus on the prose of mortality: 'There is Lockhart on the death of Scott, and Colonel Henderson on the death of Stonewall Jackson. There is the last paragraph of Thomas Hardy's *Woodlanders,* and not least is Emily Brontë: "I lingered round them under that benign sky; watched the moths fluttering among the heath and the harebells, listened to the soft wind breathing through the grass, and wondered how anyone could ever imagine unquiet slumbers for sleepers in that quiet earth." '

Surely it was of himself, as well as of Sir Edward Leithen, that he was speaking in the last sentence of *Mountain Meadow*, written a month before: 'He knew that he would die; but he knew also that he would live.'

PORTRAIT OF A FATHER

CHAPTER 21 ~

Books

A READER OF THE FIRST DRAFT of this narrative, which contained no chapter on books, complained of 'the omission of continuity in reading' — I had thought there was nothing else but — and fiercely demanded, 'How do you know what you know?' I replied evasively with a quotation and a question. 'Que sçais-je?' What do I know? I only know what I think, and that seems to arrive as the result of a life-long debate between reading and experience. When we are young we read with excitement and wonder, to find out and forecast; experience is all ahead of us. As it comes, our mood changes; we read for pleasure and participation, sometimes for mere relaxation and change. In the third stage, when experience is x per cent behind us, we read for memory and recognition. To check the books by experience, experience by the books. To add up the profit and loss of the years into the final grand balance sheet.

The contents of the library in the old house on the Bay Road, that I swallowed imperfectly chewed, has already been catalogued. My adolescent mind was a welter of romantic sentiments and Great-aunt Amanda's brand of history; but it was a kingdom of escape from loneliness and the daily oppressions of Aunt Abigail. On that insecure foundation, Winch piled the British poets, Woodberry the European epics, but these I soon began to balance with solider stuff, books like Spedding's Bacon, Jowett's Plato, Fraser's *Golden Bough,* standard and current literature and history in French and English. Until manuscripts had to be given the right of way over books, I read all the printed matter I could lay my hands on. I could even, if storm-bound in some fishing station, pass the time with *biblia abiblia,* as John Fiske calls them; encyclopaedias, dictionaries, old schoolbooks, almanacs, local histories, company reports, catalogues, statistics, country newspapers. Nothing printed save stray numbers of popular magazines and old sermons seemed alien to me. I remember the thrill I felt in discovering the birthrate of Quebec, the war of secession in Coos County, New Hampshire, in 1835, and a myriad other odd but not unrelated facts.

In the twenty years from 1910 to 1930, I read in manuscript all the books we published except Westerns and juveniles, and many that we didn't, and agreed with Cervantes that no book is so bad that one can't find something in it. I tried to keep up with the best offerings of our competitors, but printed matter came to be selected more and more for pleasure and escape.

I found it a good idea to devote spare time, if any, for a summer or a winter, to the reading or re-reading of some long set of books, filling in the background with the author's biography. Following this plan, I read at various times through Scott, Jane Austen, the Brontës, Hakluyt's *Voyages,* Stevenson, Anatole France, Fielding, Smollett, Sterne, Casanova, Boswell's Johnson, Gibbon, Trollope — the Parlia-

mentary novels more often than the Barchester series —
Proust in French as the individual volumes came out, and in
the admirable English version when they were collected. Of
the novels of Thackeray, Dickens, Hardy, Meredith, Howells,
and James, I never got through more than one or two at a
time. It sounds like a lot of reading, but a real reader like
Gamaliel Bradford could have multiplied it by a hundred.

For perfect pleasure and escape, I have found nothing better than the sixteen volumes of *The Arabian Nights* in the
Madrus French translation, a very different book from the
chastened version I read at the Lake in the previous century.
It seems to me to offer more varieties of entertainment than
any other book outside of the works of Shakespeare. It is an
omnibus of wonder, horror, romance, innocent and otherwise, tragedy, comedy, farce, extravaganza, sceptical philosophy, practical ethics, cultural history, homely wisdom,
humor, wit, and poetry. For the leisurely re-reader, the
Madrus version is incomparably the best. Burton is a little
harsh and unmodulated. The blue passages tend to 'thump,'
as painters say of an unnatural or too intense a color. Perhaps he was habitually embarrassed by the monitory image
of Lady Burton. In Madrus, a perfect Gallic naturalness
covers and excuses all. The limpid and musical French seems
to fall from the lips of Scheherezade; or, in heightened passages, from under the baton of Rimsky-Korsakov.

Through the toilsome thirties, trying to ride two mettle-
some horses at once, I became, I regret to say, an inordinate
consumer of murder-mystery stories. I never seemed to care
greatly who done it, but the lurid direct action and tough
talk seemed to be exactly what the doctor ordered to soothe
a tired business man, worn out by his endeavors to establish
the equilibrium of the heterogeneous. Some of them, like the

books of Dorothy Sayers, gave a richer pleasure than that of mere vicarious homicide. The new fishing books that came over each year from England, with peaceful pages about the uncommunicating muteness of fishes, helped to balance the hasty ration.

On country weekends and long journeys by boat or train, I still found time to read more important books, notably the sound and illuminating volumes of criticism of past and present American literature that were coming from the press and the new naturalistic novels, marked, some of them, by a range of imagination and a torrent of rhetoric that made the naturalism of the French, even some of the Russians, seem arid and thin. On one of the great days of a longish reading life, while sliding through the pine woods and tobacco fields of Virginia and North Carolina, I began and finished Thomas Wolfe's *Look Homeward, Angel.*

Now that there is more time for vagrom reading, I find myself returning to the classics as bedside books, not for the drowsy evening but for the fresh and lucid morning; for that hour before breakfast that is so much the best hour of the day. The perfect dawn patrol consists of those three guardsmen of the inquiring mind, Emerson, Plutarch, Montaigne. Experience has amply checked and confirmed their wisdom and their *savoir-faire* of the good life.

Emerson in the Winch and Woodberry days did not powerfully attract me. His Over-Soul seemed remote from men's business and bosoms. His bust, that has looked down on me for forty years from the top of the bookshelves in my room on Park Street, was not sympathetic. But now, after reading him afresh in the light of experience, that skied effigy has become the face of a friend. High-minded, yes, but shrewdly, humanly wise in the conduct of life. He made his publishers pay a twenty per cent royalty, not when they sold, but when they printed. On a 'bright, sharp' early spring day in 1860 he walked for two hours with Walt Whitman up and down the Long Mall, that I see out of the corner of my left eye as I write these words, debating the inclusion of Children of Adam in the forthcoming Boston edition of the *Leaves of Grass*. His objections to the 'outcast pieces' were, Walt tells us, 'neither moral nor literary, but given with a view to my worldly success.'

It was his *Journals* that first revealed to me the true Emerson, always quietly humorous in phrase as in his view of the actions of men. The discovery gave a new warmth to his *English Traits* and *Representative Men*, his two best books, and I know few better.

Plutarch's *Lives* and *Morals* were known to me only in extracts until the day a few years ago that I purchased a nobly printed set of the latter in Henry Morgan's eighteenth-century translation. On my library table, it opened automatically at a page containing the casual statement, 'A fishing rod should be strong enough to resist the jerks of the fish when he is hooked, but not so stout as to cast a shadow to scare him away.' It was a nice point, expressed in words that revealed the expert angler. I had a new fishing friend.

The delighted sense of recognition brought me by the five volumes of the *Morals* took me back to the *Lives*. There, in the balanced 'characters' of the prepotent men of two civilizations, I found a certified account of the world's experience for half a millennium, the perfect preparation for the arrival of the morning paper with the news from Washington, London, Moscow, and Chungking.

Montaigne, first tasted on Morningside as a corrective for

an overdose of idealism, is the best companion of all for that pre-breakfast tour. Surely Florio's translation lay beside Shakespeare's own bed, not that 'second-best' piece of furniture he willed to his wife. For me Charles Cotton, another fishing fellow, has produced the English version that in its colloquial simplicity and just sufficient patine of antiquity comes closest to the original. But it is well to read an *Essay* every now and then in the author's own not too difficult French.

In whichever language I read him, he seems the perfect pattern of the reasonable man: as full of respect for others as for himself, with humility as well as pride of intellect, gay in manner, serious of heart, eager for pleasure, yet never forgetful of duty. He took for his guide, as he says, 'the ways of the world and the experience of the senses.' Standing like a buffer state between the static right and the dynamic left, he was distrusted by both; by the right for his questioning curiosities, by the left for his tolerance of the right. So have I found the gentlemen of the left better for the high ridge walks of speculation, the men of the right to do business and fish with.

To poetry, although my mind is stored, perhaps cluttered, with its tags, I am less susceptible than of old. Few modern poets have penetrated me very deeply. The drumbeat of the stavic alliteration of MacLeish's *Conquistador* moves me more than the rhythm of any other recent verse, and for meaning, Rainer Maria Rilke rewards study better than any of his contemporaries. His elucidators seem to me at times to have obscured, if not confused, his thought. My German is not too capable, but it helps me to meet his subtle and passionate mind better than many of the translations.

The concluding couplet of his last Sonnet to Orpheus, which I have set on the title page of this book, is the perfect stream fisherman's epitaph:

> Zu der stillen Erde sag: Ich rinne.
> Zu dem raschen Wasser sprich: Ich bin.

CHAPTER 22

Feller in the creek

PERHAPS THE REASON I have brought so eager a passion to the fishing of so many rivers is that I have never had enough of it. Three times in forty years I have taken a full month off just to fish, once in County Cork, once in the Cévennes, once on the far isle of Anticosti. Apart from those halcyon cycles of the moon, my fishing has always been over long weekends, or, at best, two weekends with the week between; never so far away that telegrams, or the telephone plus swift-footed messenger, couldn't catch up and keep me in touch with work.

On the other hand, as Lord Grey says in his *Fly Fishing,* 'work, if it be of an interesting sort and not crushing in amount, is a fine preparation for the country. Such work is stimulating, and when we make our escape, we do it with faculties erect and active, with every sense alert and eager for sights and sounds and all joys which are not to be met with in cities.'

It was during the Dividend and Laocoön decades that such escapes brought the most tingling pleasure. The truth is that in those years I seemed to have become a schizo personality, fifty per cent executive and factual, the other moiety literary and fanciful. There was a civil war in my innards for which

I could negotiate no peace save when wading in the river
with the fish, sharing their cold, sweet, silver life, becoming
for bird and kine and native passer-by merely a harmless
'feller in the creek.'

Considering the temporal limitation, I am not ill content
with the spatial expanse drained by the streams I have fished.
If a catalogue of ships, why not one of rivers?

In New York: the Upper Hudson, Gansevoort Creek,
known to Herman Melville and his Pierre, and the Halfway
Brook of my own first emprises; later the Ausable, the Aeso-
pus, Kinderhook Creek, the Willowemoc, the Beaverkill, the
Neversink with Edward Hewitt performing prodigies of rolling casts, the Callicoon with George La Branche darting
upstream like a swallow, creating artificial hatches, taking
plump pounders from the most unpromising places.

In Massachusetts: the Konkopot, the Swift, and the three
branches of the Westfield. In Connecticut: the Blackberry
and the Eight Mile River, rising in that Devil's Hop Yard of
Old Lyme, where, in colonial days, young men and maidens
hopped in secret midnight dances, an American Witchwood.
In Rhode Island: Queen's River, where Grant La Farge at
seventy reached the top of a pine tree like a panther to de-
tach his companion's fly from a reluctant cone.

In Vermont, where in all the winding valleys rail and road
and river are braided together and tied at their nodes by
covered bridges: the Walloomsac, West River, White River,
Otter Creek, the Barton, the Nulhegin, and the Battenkill,

> Strong without rage, without e'er flowing full.

In New Hampshire: the Pine, the Smith, the Baker, the
Saco, the Wildcat, the Glen Ellis; Connor's River, where, on
leaving the stream, I surprised an Arcadian idyll in full

bloom under an apple tree; the stony Peabody, the terraced Connecticut, the loggy Androscoggin; the thin Mohawk, the Double Diamond, three Swifts, the Ammonoosuc, the Wild Ammonoosuc, the Upper Ammonoosuc, and the Beebe.

On the last, I had a part in the performance of a miracle of the fishes.

One day with a friend I drove for five miles over the bumpy right of way of a lumber railroad in process of construction into the secret heart of the Sandwich Range. After some hours of bushy fishing, we brought to net an iridescent monstrosity of a rainbow trout. Only thirteen inches long, he must have weighed well toward two pounds. Anyone beholding him would have said, with the slightly elevated gentleman in *Punch* swaying before an enormous stuffed trout in a glass case, 'The man that caught that fish is a liar!' On our way out to the car we saw by the side of the trail a rusty motorcycle. Hanging from the handlebars was a small fish basket; no fisherman in sight. In the basket, which we were moved to investigate, was an emaciated little trout the size of your middle finger, a good two inches under the limit. Throwing this into the bushes, we forced leviathan into its place in the basket, completely filling it. Some unknown Brother of the Angle has a tale to tell.

In Maine, I have fished the Cambridge, the Magalloway, the Cupsuptic, Rapid River (a five-pounder to the little Iron Blue), Sandy River, Dead River, Moose River, Misere Stream (seventy-two in a week, averaging better than two pounds, all to the dry fly), Brassua Stream; the various branches of the Penobscot, the Sourdnahunk, the Narragaugus, the Machias, the Denys; the thoroughfares of the Fish River Chain; most often and, with the Connecticut, best loved of all, Kennebago Stream.

Along the twelve miles of that delightful water ran the abandoned line of a railway, over which a road bus with flanged wheels and miniature freight car behind for guides and rods and fish transported me in luxury, down in the morning, back at night. In the mid-thirties, the rails were taken up and sold, despite my warnings of their evil designs, to the Japs to blow us up with. Thereafter, I have fished only as many of the thirty pools between the Falls and Indian Rock as I thought my legs would get me back from. The eighteenth pool, one of the loveliest, with the pyramid of Kennebago Mountain exactly on its upstream axis, is now called Drinkwater's Bath, from what happened to that agreeable poet when, contrary to the most explicit instructions from a more cautious adventurer, he endeavored to lengthen his cast by mounting a large stone known to be of the type that gathers no moss.

In North Carolina: the Nantahala and Hazel Run, high in the Great Smokies, where the feller in the creek had intimate conversations with fellow fishermen, white and colored. Florida rivers hardly count, but the fly-taking bass and spotted weakfish of the St. Lucie, Anclote, and Homosassa are a pleasant *ersatz* memory.

In Ireland: The Blackwater, Awbeg, Araglin, North Bride, where Jim White, as the water rose over his waders, chanted, 'Here comes the Bride,' and the Funshion, on which, under the ruined walls of Glanworth, I in a dinner jacket, having eaten and drunk deep of Irish hospitality, essayed to show a salmon fisher from home, who said he had never seen it done, how a trout was taken on a floating fly. A bad mess I made of it, too, until dinner wore off; and between eleven and eleven-fifteen in the late northern twilight, the priest was put to a brace of good trout. A mile or two on any river in the truly emerald isle will teach you more of Irish history than all the books. At every bend is a ruined tower. There lived large Irish families, with all their cousins, descendants of ancient kings, that made merry wars and sad songs, and developed the fiery individualism that is at once their charm and their undoing.

In France: the Truyère, the Haute Loire at Goudet, where I arrived after a twenty-mile drive from Le Puy with only one wader; and the green translucent Tarn. In Canada, where also a fly is a *mouche* and the reel a *moulin,* the Batiscon, the Rivière Noire, Jacques Cartier, Cassein, Rivière des Neiges, and Montmorency. In Anticosti, still in the same language, the Jupiter, the Becsie, the St. Marie, and the Canard. *En route* to the lastnamed, I complained to the *gardien* of the snail's pace of the white stallion that was inching us along a boggy lumber road. Said the *gardien,* 'You don't understand; this is the father of all the horses on the island.' Said I, 'Peut-être il est mieux pour l'amour que pour le voyage!' The steed laid his ears back and looked around with a mean expression. The *injure* rankled in his slow equine mind. When we left the river with two satisfactory salmon and came to the ruined lumber camp where the conveyance had been left, there it was, but — no horse! Following the track of stately hoofprints, I walked the nine miles to Port Menier in waders and the rain, resolved in the future to try to guard my tongue.

The roll of the rivers of England has been called in another chapter. It is the anglers' terrestrial paradise where the fishing seems to get better and better with the years. It was noted in a monastery record of the twelfth century that it wasn't what it used to be, but today a century of steady stocking and preserving seems to have turned the curve the other way. There in weedy gin-clear waters, flowing over white beds of gravel, I saw that Shakespeare knew what he was talking about when he wrote in *Much Ado,*

> The pleasantest angling is to see the fish
> Cut with her golden oars the silver stream.

Of these fourscore rivers, I remember not only the pools and runs, but the best methods of approaching them and the actual lie of the fish. On nights when care-charming sleep will not be wooed to my bed, I count no silly sheep, but fish a mile or two of selected river, downstream wet or upstream dry, as suits my mood. Always I drop off, and sometimes finish out the stretch in sleep. But the fish we hook in dreams rarely reaches the net.

There are other streams that I have only day-dreamed of fishing: Michigan's Père Marquette, Idaho's Northwest Snake, Oregon's Rogue, British Columbia's Kamloops; the rivers of Princess Charlotte Island, stiff with great free-rising Pacific salmon, the Scotch-like waters of Tasmania, the angler's paradise in the Chilean Andes, the Erste and Hex rivers of South Africa advertised by John Buchan, New Zealand's Tongariro, mouth-filling name, in accord with the net-filling rainbows it produces.

I had hoped, when Anno Domini had done her work and purely publishing adventures swung full circle, to cast a fly on some of these distant waters. My purpose still holds to sail beyond the sunset after the war, but South Africa and Tasmania begin to look like Carcassonnes.

> How dull it is to pause, to make an end,
> To rust unburnish'd, not to shine in use!

The choice of fishing companions is a deep matter. In camp, for bridge or dominoes in the evening, three are all right, but on the water one is enough, and, unless rating at least ninety on a scale of one hundred, too many. A wife or daughter, or what you have, who takes an intelligent interest in the proceedings, who appreciates your merit without emulation, and is not bored when you expound it to her, who likes fish to eat, is an excellent fellow traveller. Of your own sex, the ideal is someone who is not only keen and competent, but curious, reflective, well read in the literature of the subject, who considers fishing not a competitive sport but a branch of philosophy, who takes as much pleasure in your fish as you do in his. Of my own preferred companions, a majority have been surgeons or painters — neat-handed, individualistic, free-minded fellows, like Bob Greenough, *beau joueur* at every outdoor and indoor sport, lord of the Seigneurie of Pertuis in the Laurentians, who fought the battle of public health against the cancer foe till his own untimely death. *Par excellence*, I'd choose Leslie Thompson, distinguished painter and fishing philosopher, master of the useful art of camouflaging quick thinking behind slow speech. I have fished, or discoursed of fishing, with the chief angling authorities of our time — Lord Grey, Sheringham, Skues, Hewitt, La Branche — but have known no more knowledgable head and cunning hand than Lett's, no companion who so consistently doubles streamside joys and halves the griefs.

Of guides and gillies, a book could be written. Two would deserve a chapter apiece, Jim O'Brien, of the Kennebago, guide, philosopher, naturalist, stream-strategist, friend; and Jack O'Brien, of the Cork Blackwater, incomparable raconteur.

One day, during a mixed party of happy memory at Castle Hyde, near Fermoy, the men went for the day to some hope-

ful salmon water downstream. There Jack O'Brien, octogenarian, tall, ruddy-cheeked, taciturn, took us in charge.
From the stratospherical point of view, Ireland is but a green
speck in the Atlantic Ocean. So it is, too, from the meteoro-
logical, and we were having that day quite a spot of Atlantic
weather. We worked downstream — three casts, three steps
forward, three more casts, three steps forward, and so on
da capo. I did it in three-four time, to the melody of 'Casey
would waltz with the strawberry blonde'; at every step the
rain in the back of my neck got colder. The seely salmon
hugged the bottom where it was warm. Topside it was a
blank and chilling forenoon.

At lunchtime, the ladies of the party arrived on the drip-
ping scene with a hamper. From it appeared a roast duck, a
whole ham with fixings, two bottles of Burgundy, six of Bass,
and one of John Jameson. As the last was handed out, I
descried a dotted line straight to it from O'Brien's faded eye:

'Would you like a drink, O'Brien?'

'I would, sir!'

Taking a water tumbler, he filled it seven-eighths full of
the creature, put it down the hatch in two gulps and became
suddenly loquacious:

'Sure and it's strange things that happen on this Blackwater River, and the strangest I ever seen was right by yon
tree, in 1872, it was, in February.

'I was spinning for pike. I was casting it out and reeling it
in, and casting it out and reeling it in, and of a sudden I
heard the sound of the hunting horn. And I looked over
there across the river, and round that little hill there I seen
the fox coming, and after him the hounds, and the master,
and the beautiful gentlemen and ladies on their great beautiful horses.

'And the fox he jumped in the river and started swimming this way, and the hounds after him, and the gentlemen and ladies wading their horses up there by the stickle.

'And the fox he got halfway across and then he sank from sight; and I said to meself, "Alas, the fox, poor fellow, he's drowned!"

'And just then I felt a big pull on me spinning rig, a great pike it was that weighed forty-three pounds, and I played him up and I played him down, and at last I got the gaff into him, and I pulled him out on the bank and hit him three, no, 'twas four times, on the head with me priest.

'And I turned him over, and there was his belly bulging out like nothing you ever saw before. And I says to meself, "Sure and it's funny the way that pike's belly sticks out," and I took out me knife and slit him up the belly.

'And out jumps the fox, and he ran three miles before they killed him.'

It is a far cry from an Irish fish story to the poetry of Wordsworth, but each year in August or September, after a summer of heat and stale air in town, on the Connecticut or Kennebago stream, I enjoy an experience that is pure Wordsworth. Lord Grey had it, too, in pursuit of the sea-trout in Scotland, and set it down in words too perfect for paraphrase:

'The difference is so great in August, after a few days of exercise in the air of the North, that there come times when the angler, who wanders alone after sea-trout down glens and over moors, has a sense of physical energy and strength beyond all his experience in ordinary life. Often after walking a mile or two on the way to the river, at a brisk pace, there comes upon one a feeling of "fitness," of being made of nothing but health and strength so perfect, that life need have no other end but to enjoy them. It is as though till that moment one had breathed with only a part of one's lungs, and as though now for the first time the whole lungs were filling with air. The pure act of breathing at such times seems glorious. People talk of being a child of nature, and moments such as these are the times when it is possible to feel so; to know the full joy of animal life — to desire nothing beyond. There are times when I have stood still for joy of it all, on my way through the wild freedom of a Highland moor, and felt the wind, and looked upon the mountains and water and light and sky, till I felt conscious only of the strength of a mighty current of life, which swept away all consciousness of self, and made me a part of all that I beheld.'

That is the mystical aspect of fishing. Schubert has reproduced its music in the notes of the *Müllerlieder:*

> Ich hört ein Bächlein rauschen
> Wohl aus dem Felsingwell
> Hinab zum Thale rauschen
> So frisch und wunderhell.

The mood of the actual fishing is the same everywhere. It is always a restrained and muted fierceness. It is in the casting of the fly, when a moment's languor is fatal: in the striking and playing of the fish. It is the source of numberless acts of unrecorded heroism, as when rheumatic old men deliberately go over their waders to cover a rising fish without drag. It is a fire in the heart that drives us on to one more pool long after we are thoroughly exhausted and reprehensibly late for supper. The Indians knew it as they cast their buck tails on wilderness waters, and my Great-uncle Charles, God rest him, who caught his death wading in the brook on his eightieth birthday, felt its propelling urge. In short, it is fishing.

And of fishing, the fly rod is the characteristic implement and perfect symbol. I have three, in especial, baptized in trout water with the names of the fathers and mother of the church, Izaak, Sir Henry, Dame Juliana. How their yielding resiliency typifies the character of the great men who have graced our annals, and of many a mute inglorious fisherman, too! What magical comfort comes on winter nights, when the world and its unreason have been too much with us, from the mere handling of their shining strength! When spring is not far behind and trout begin to cast an upward eye, and city-pent fishermen make strange passes with their walking sticks, it is my habit to set a bundle of three or four rods and a net handle in some conspicuous position where the eye will fall frequently on it. That precious roll is the emblem of a gentler fascism than the sons of Caesar have represented by their bundle of stolid staves. It stands for direct action presently to come, for memories of vanished days, and for enduring friendship with kindred minds, companions along the rivers of home and by streams beyond the once estranging sea.

And what of the River of Life, the springs whence it comes and the sea where it goes?

An English friend, G. E. M. Skues, has written a classic fishing book, *Minor Tactics of the Chalk Stream.* Minor tactics have their place on the turbid stream of consciousness, too. It is the little things that make up the good day. The scent of a country morning; a catbird's phrase; a line of verse or a page of prose; some small mirth-making incongruity, a happily found word for a quaint conceit; the warm presence of a friend, a responsive smile; the light of sun or moon or star; or, if the weather turns sour, the dash of rain in your face.

Nor is this the supine philosophy of a new beatitude. Minor tactics are active, not passive. They succeed only at the hands of the persistent and alert. As in fishing, languor is fatal.

And when the great fish is seen to rise, forty pounds of salmon, silver-fresh from the sea, and you with only your trout rod; why, then James Graham, Earl of Montrose, had the right idea,

> He either fears his fate too much,
> Or his deserts are small,
> Who dares not put it to the touch
> To gain or lose it all.

Yet 'gain or lose,' who can say what they mean? Perhaps all living is just learning the meaning of words; not the sesquipedalians that we look up in the dictionary, but the big one-syllable basic words that are fully defined only in the lexicon of experience: 'work and play,' 'joy and pain'; 'peace,' 'love,' 'life' itself — and 'death' its silent inevitable companion. Their meanings, alas! we master too late to employ completely. The learning is all.

THE END

INDEX